W9-AYR-374

NORTH CAROLINA
CRAFT BEER & BREWERIES

NORTH CAROLINA CRAFT BEER & BREWERIES

ERIK LARS MYERS

JOHN F. BLAIR, PUBLISHER   WINSTON-SALEM, NORTH CAROLINA

Published by

JOHN F. BLAIR
P U B L I S H E R
1406 Plaza Drive
Winston-Salem, North Carolina 27103
www.blairpub.com

COVER IMAGE

Copyright FikMik, 2011, used under license from Shutterstock.com

Cover design by Angela Harwood
Interior by Debra Long Hampton and Melissa Clark James

Photo on Frontispiece: Barrels at Olde Hickory Brewery

Library of Congress Cataloging-in-Publication Data

Myers, Erik Lars.
  North Carolina craft beer & breweries / by Erik Lars Myers.
    p. cm.
  Includes index.
  ISBN 978-0-89587-571-6 (alk. paper) — ISBN 978-0-89587-572-3 (ebook)
  1. Beer—North Carolina. 2. Breweries—North Carolina. I. Title. II. Title:
North Carolina craft beer and breweries.
  TP577.M94 2012
  338.7'6634209756--dc23
                        2011052574

10 9 8 7 6 5 4 3 2 1

Contents

THE MOUNTAINS

THE PIEDMONT

THE TRIANGLE

THE COAST

A brewer hard at work at Catawba Valley Brewing Company

Preface

- - - - - - - - - -

This is an exciting time to be a fan of craft beer in North Carolina. It hasn't always been this way. As you'll see in the following pages, North Carolina does not have a long and storied brewing history, though beer has been in the state for as long as people have. Even considering the large influx of British, Scottish, German, and Czech immigrants, North Carolina has no giant brewing center—no Philadelphia, Milwaukee, or St. Louis. It does not have the perfect climate for growing barley or hops. It has not always boasted a friendly political climate for alcohol.

Today, thanks in no small part to 2005's Pop the Cap bill (see pages 191-92), North Carolina has one of the most exciting and dynamic emerging beer cultures in the country. It is a leader in the craft beer industry, claiming more breweries and more national and international awards than any other state in the American South. North Carolina is quickly becoming recognized as having some of the most sought-after beers and breweries in the country.

What's more, North Carolina brewers are compatriots before they are competitors. They are congenial, friendly, and helpful to one another. That same warm camaraderie is reflected in the patrons—the state's beer lovers and homebrewers. To put it simply, North Carolina is a great place to have a beer.

In this book, I hope to show the essence of the craft beer community in the state. Like that of any small business, the true story of a brewery is not its label art or its logo, but the people behind it. Small craft breweries are labors of love. Their proprietors are passionate and driven, and the beers they produce often reflect their personalities. To know a craft brewer is to know his or her beer.

In each profile, I try to capture the people behind the brewery and the beer, in order to show the diverse population that gets itself into the brewing industry. Breweries are complex entities. No two are alike. The smallest brewery in North Carolina makes 10 gallons of beer at a time and produced approximately 500 gallons in 2011. The largest brewery in the state produced somewhere around 15,000 barrels, or 465,000 gallons. To consider those two businesses as parts of the same industry seems almost ludicrous, yet they're cut from the same cloth. Both were built by passionate homebrewers who wanted to take their craft to the next level simply because they love great beer and want to share it with others.

It's my goal to present those people to you.

Astute North Carolina craft beer fans may notice the conspicuous absence of Charlotte's Rock Bottom Brewery from the book. Rock Bottom, now owned by Gordon Biersch, is the only national chain brewpub left in the state. Because of the book's focus on the people behind the breweries and the emphasis on local breweries, I elected to leave Rock Bottom off the list. However, as you partake of beer tourism around the state, I encourage you to stop by Rock Bottom and have a pint. It might not be a local brewery from a management and ownership perspective, but the people who work there are local and are just as passionate about beer as those at any other North Carolina brewery. They'll appreciate your business.

Unfortunately, it's almost impossible to write a book about beer in North Carolina and keep it up to date. At the time of this writing, more than a dozen breweries were in the process of opening around the state, and more are being planned every day. Many of those startups are listed in Appendix 1. Be sure to keep an eye out for them. They are the future of the industry just as much as the veteran brewers.

I hope this book inspires you to support your local North Carolina brewery and to experience beer from around the state. With the right help, the beer industry can continue its growth and become an economic boon to North Carolina's agriculture, tourism, and hospitality industries. That help is you. Your presence, your support, and your passion can make North Carolina beer and breweries flourish for years to come.

Acknowledgments

For his friendship, for suggesting me as a possible author for this book, and for providing the base for what became the North Carolina beer history timeline, I thank Jonathan Surratt, proprietor of beermapping.com, a tool that should be in the back pocket of every beer tourist, and beerinator.com, a wonderful online North Carolina beer community.

Thanks to the fantastic staff at John F. Blair, Publisher, for taking a chance on an untested author and helping me through the process with professional grace, humor, and enthusiasm.

A huge thank-you to the North Carolina craft beer community, from brewers to drinkers to everyone in between. The enthusiasm and drive that all of you show are both inspiring and humbling. I would especially like to thank Sebastian Wolfrum of Natty Greene's and Sean Lily Wilson of Fullsteam for their friendship, unending support, and passion for North Carolina beer.

I offer thanks to John Schlick, Adam Rowe, Sarah D'Amato, Stuart Arnold, Glenn Powlas, Larry Jones, Mike Ranck, Jim Looney, Chris Darling, Joe Mecca, Jeremy Fanning, Adam Ledford, Daniel McKinnin, and Jon Odgers for help in tracking down bottle shops around North Carolina.

Thanks to my left hand, assistant brewer, and good friend Chris Shields for compiling an enormous amount of the information in these pages and especially for taking some of the pressure of starting Mystery Brewing Company off my shoulders while I finished the book.

No amount of thanks could possibly be enough for my lovely wife, Sarah Ficke, who spent hours combing through historical documents, even more hours being the first reader on the book, and still more hours putting up with me while I worked on it. I could not do this—or anything—without her.

Single Brothers' Brewery and Distillery in Salem
PHOTO COURTESY OF OLD SALEM MUSEUMS AND GARDENS

A History of North Carolina Beer and Brewing

Traditional histories of North Carolina say little or no brewing was done in the state's past. They cite the warm, humid climate and ignore the generations of British, Scottish, German, and Czech immigrants who settled North Carolina. Having arrived from beer-drinking cultures, those immigrants were unlikely to forgo their favorite beverage simply because of a little weather.

However, North Carolina's beer history is significantly more complicated than that of beer-producing states in the North like Pennsylvania and New York. Early on, barley was difficult to grow in North Carolina, and many traditional brewing ingredients had to be imported or improvised. The Revolutionary War and the Civil War both had significant impacts on ingredient availability and imports. Then came our country-wide "Noble Experiment": Prohibition.

Through it all, in just 200 years, North Carolina has gone from being one of the lowest beer-producing states to the heart of the southeastern beer market and one of the most exciting emerging beer scenes in the country.

Brewing in the Colonial Period

Brewing has been practiced in North Carolina since the early days of the colony. Christoph von Graffenried included in his *Account of the Founding of New Bern* (the town was founded in 1710) a letter from a colonist to a kinsman in Germany requesting that he send brewing equipment "because my wife understands brewing so well and has done it for years, and the drink is very scarce here."[1]

John Brickell, an Irishman who traveled in North Carolina between 1729 and 1731, published a book called *Natural History of North Carolina* in 1737. In it, he reported on the popularity of beer, imported rum, brandy, and "Mault Drink." According to Brickell, "The following are made in Country, viz. Cyder, Persimon-Beer, made of the Fruit of that Tree, Ceder-Beer, made of Ceder-Berries; they also make Beer of the green stalks of Indian-Corn, which they bruise and boyle. They likewise make Beer of Mollosses, or common Treacle, in the following manner, they take a Gallon of Mollosses, a Peck of Wheaten Bran, a Pound of Hops, and a Barrel of Fountain Water, all which they boile together, and work up with Yest, as we do our Malt Liquors; this is their common Small-Beer, and seems to me to be the pleasantest Drink, I ever tasted, either in the Indies or Europe, and I am satisfied more wholsom. This is made stronger in proportion, as People fancy."[2]

Brickell noted that traditional brewing was not widespread: "It is necessary to observe that though there is plenty of Barly and Oats in this Province, yet there is no Malt Drink made, notwithstanding all kind of Malt Liquors bear a good Price, nor have any of the Planters ever yet attempted it."[3]

Some evidence suggests that larger-scale brewing existed in the colony as well. When the town of Cross Creek in Cumberland County (now part of Fayetteville) was mapped in 1770, a brewery was one of the buildings marked on it.[4] A brewery was also a key part of the town of Salem, founded by the Moravians, early immigrants to North Carolina with a Czech background. The Single Brothers—as the unmarried Moravian men were called—ran several industries in town, including a brewery, which existed from 1774 to 1813.[5]

However, histories also report almost unanimously that the climate in the Southern colonies was not ideal for growing barley. The heat was cited as causing storage problems. In *Brewed in America: A History of Beer and Ale in the United States*, author Stanley Baron noted that farmers experimented with growing barley and hops in the Carolinas and that "the usual home brewing" took place, but that "rum is supposed to have taken over here particularly early and thus reduced the beer requirements."[6]

What were Carolinians really drinking during the colonial period? Rum was certainly popular, but pricing lists for taverns in that period show that they also carried a variety of beers, including "strong malt beer of America," "strong malt beer of Britain," and "British ale or beer bottled and wired in Great Britain," as well as both "Northern" and "Carolina" ciders. Carolina cider was the least expensive of those drinks per quart, and a beer "bottled and wired in Great Britain" was the most expensive by far.[7] The histories report that most beer in the Southern colonies was imported either from the North or from Britain. In fact, Baron's book explains that refusing to import beer from Britain was one step the Americans took during the Revolutionary War to break with the mother country.

From the Revolutionary War to the Civil War

Brewing continued in North Carolina after the Revolutionary War, both at home and on a larger scale. William Lenoir's plantation distilling book, kept from 1806 to 1808, included instructions on malting barley and a recipe for making three kinds of beer (strong beer, middle beer, and small beer), to be brewed in one session using the same grain for all three beers.[8] In 1807, Henry Gunnisson used the *Wilmington Gazette* to announce that he had started a brewery "in Wilkinson's Alley, on the West side of Front Street"—just a few blocks from where Wilmington's Front Street Brewery stands today.[9]

The North Carolina brewer most active in the newspapers during this period was Thomas Holmes of Salisbury, who ran a series of advertisements in the *Western Carolinian*. Holmes announced that he was opening a public house in October 1821. By December 1822, he was advertising for barley for his brewery. In April 1823, he opened a "new establishment . . . where he intends to keep a constant supply of Beer and Porter."[10] Holmes encouraged local production of brewing ingredients. In June 1823, he advertised for hops "for which he will pay 30 cents pr. Pound, if picked in a good season, when not too dry."[11] He also encouraged people to drink local beer over liquor. Holmes continued to run periodic advertisements until the spring of 1827, when he announced he was returning to a former location in town to run a "house of entertainment."[12] At that point, he and his brewery dropped out of the newspaper records. However, the August 19, 1828, edition of the *Western Carolinian* reported that "a highly respectable and enterprising gentleman of Salisbury, fitted up a Brewery here about a year since; and was in the 'full tide of successful experiment,' when lately his principal workman, an experienced brewer, died, and the operations of the brewery had consequently to be suspended for a time." In a burst of local pride, the paper added that "the Beer and Porter produced at this establishment, was superior to any liquor of the kind ever manufactured in this part of the country; it was getting to be generally used by our citizens, and promised to have a salutary tendency to check the excessive use of ardent spirits."[13] The article did not name names, though, so the connection between this brewery and the one run by Thomas Holmes is unknown.

Although small-scale brewing was practiced in North Carolina during the first half of the 19th century, it was not enough to register in the national histories of the industry. *One Hundred Years of Brewing*, a history and collection of 19th-century brewing statistics published in 1903 and sponsored by the trade journal *Western Brewer*, didn't mention any breweries south of Maryland and Washington, D.C., in its pre–Civil War section.

The comparatively small amount of North Carolina–brewed beer during this period didn't mean people weren't drinking it. While rum and whiskey were definitely popular, so was beer, but it was often imported from other states or Europe. North Carolina newspaper articles from the post–Revolutionary War period contained advertisements from stores selling bottled and casked porter from England, barrels of porter from Philadelphia, ale from Albany, and "Scotch ale."

When North Carolinians made beer, it often stretched the boundaries of what might be considered beer today. While they did make traditional English ales out of barley malt, hops, yeast, and water, a wide variety of recipes from the early 19th century involved many more ingredients—everything from other types of grain or corn to herbs, fruits, spruce, extra sugars, and even raw eggs. Based on recipes published in newspapers and other publications at the time, most homebrewed beer in North Carolina was table beer, meant to be a refreshing, low-alcohol beverage served regularly at meals.

In August 1828, the *Western Carolinian* offered this recipe: "The following ingredients make a palatable and healthy table beer; take 3 lbs. sugar or molasses, 1 gallon wheat bran, and 3 ozs. hops; put them into 4 gals. water, boil it three quarters of an hour, strain the liquor through a sieve, put it in a cool place a short time, then into a cask, and add six gals. of cold water, and put in half a pint of yeast. After it works, it will be an excellent beverage, better than whiskey, brandy, rum, gin, wine, cider, or ale."[14]

In July 1847, the *Carolina Watchman* concluded its article on what farmers should drink out in the fields with a recipe for "Chinese Beer." The beer contained "spices," lemon, cream of tartar, sugar, and one bottle of "old porter."[15]

Molasses seems to have been a popular ingredient in early beer recipes, sometimes providing most of the fermentable sugar. This fits with the idea that barley malt was hard to come by in the Carolinas. Though it certainly existed, it may not have been available in the quantity needed to make a lot of beer—an issue that lingers today.

Brewing and the Civil War

The Civil War had a significant impact on North Carolina's beer brewing and consumption habits, since the state imported so much of its beer, malt, and other ingredients from the North. Tensions between North and South might have affected Southern beer as early as 1850, when the *Carolina Watchman* reprinted an article from the *Mobile Herald and Tribune* responding to some anti-Southern resolutions passed by the Massachusetts Senate. The article proposed several responses, one of which was "that we encourage Southern agriculture by giving preference to all produce cultivated in the Southern States, viz. . . . that we drink no ale, porter, or cider made in the north, but encourage the growth of Southern hops and apples, and the establishment of Southern breweries."[16]

After the war started, the Southern states did at least try to restrict beer imports. The 1861 publication *Tariff of the Confederate States of America* listed "fifteen per centum ad valorem" taxes on goods including "beer, ale, and porter, in casks or bottles,"[17] while the 1864 *Statutes at Large of the Confederate States of America* prohibited importing "beer, ale and porter."[18] Southern recipe books proposed home-brewed alternatives to imported beer. *The Confederate Receipt Book: A Compilation of Over One Hundred Receipts, Adapted to the Times* contained recipes for table beer, spruce beer, and ginger beer that all used molasses as the fermentable sugar and only sometimes used hops. The book *Resources of the Southern Fields and Forests* focused on ingredients available in the Southern states. The author included a section on how to make Russian kvass out of rye and a section on growing hops for medicinal and brewing purposes. He addressed the climate problem this way: "Ale and beer can be made in the Confederate States, though not with the same advantage as in colder climates. Though without practical experience, I am forced to the conviction that the desideratum is cool cellars. In the rural districts what are called dry cellars are constructed in the clay, just above the water-bearing stratum, the top enclosed or covered with a closed house. The temperature of these cellars is quite low, and they are used in keeping milk, butter, melons, cider, etc. I think their temperature would allow the manufacture and preservation of either wine, ale or beer."[19]

During the war, the North Carolina General Assembly gradually prohibited the making of liquor and then beer from grain, in order to protect the state's food supply.[20]

Brewing after the Civil War and the Onset of Prohibition

Beer imports rose again after the Civil War. On June 14, 1866, the *Old North State* paper advertised the sale of Cockade City Brewery beer (from Petersburg, Virginia) in Salisbury, and on November 8, 1877, the *Carolina Watchman* mentioned importing beer from the Bergner & Engle's brewery of Philadelphia. In 1890, the *Branson's North Carolina Business* directory listed beer bottlers in Tarboro, Elizabeth City, Wilson, and Fayetteville. The Robert Portner Brewing Company, based in Alexandria, Virginia, opened a bottling and storage operation in Wilmington after the war that lasted the rest of the century.

However, there is little evidence of brewing in North Carolina during this period. *One Hundred Years of Brewing* listed a few breweries for Virginia, South Carolina, Tennessee, and Georgia between 1876 and 1902, but none in North Carolina whatsoever. The book's tables listing "Production, in barrels, of malt liquors in the United States," "Summary of sales of malt liquors by states," and "Production in barrels of malt liquors in the United States" showed North Carolina as having significantly lower numbers than surrounding states. In some cases, surrounding states reported hundreds of thousands of barrels, while North Carolina had none. Virginia, Georgia, and Tennessee reported over 100,000 barrels of malt liquor (the legal term for beer at the time) for 1897 (roughly 50 times more than those states reported 100 years later). North Carolina reported zero barrels in 1897.

The enormous gap suggests a reporting issue, not just a lack of breweries. The numbers were most likely reported from Internal Revenue Service sources. The IRS starting taxing alcohol in the years immediately following the war. North Carolina, as a strong center of Confederate government, may have resisted reporting barrels (or anything else) for taxation to the IRS.

F. W. Salem's book *Beer: Its History and Its Economic Value as a National Beverage* contained more specific data about North Carolina, saying that the state had one brewery—J. W. Lancashire Brewery in Fayetteville—that sold four barrels of beer in 1878–79, a ludicrously small number. The same information can be found in William L. Downward's *Dictionary of the History of the American Brewing and Distilling Industries*. However, that book also stated that North Carolina had 273 grain distilleries with a capacity of 1,073 bushels/2,773 gallons. The sheer number of distilleries suggests that either North Carolinians really did love whiskey more than any other drink (which is possible) or that beer production occurred under the umbrella of whiskey distilling and therefore didn't show up separately in government reporting. After all, *beer* was a term frequently used to refer to the product before it was distilled. Alternately, it is possible that neighboring states produced much more grain alcohol than beer and merely reported beer production, instead of distillation, to the IRS. The fact that malting grain and making yeast for beer and whiskey were often spoken of together, as in the Lenoir plantation records, suggests the processes weren't considered wholly different from each other in the 19th century.

Another important issue in postwar North Carolina was Prohibition. Following small restriction movements in the state throughout the 19th century, efforts grew after the Civil War. In 1874, North Carolina passed the "local option" law, which allowed townships, and eventually counties, to vote to prohibit the sale of liquor. Statewide prohibition was attempted in 1881 but was defeated by popular vote. However, laws mandating more gradual implementation were passed, such as the Watts Bill (1903), which prohibited both the sale and manufacture of liquor outside incorporated towns, and the Ward Law (1905), which prohibited the manufacture of liquor in towns of fewer than 1,000 people.

The interesting thing about these early laws is their struggle to categorize beer. In a proposed 1881 law, homebrewed wines and beers would have been exempted. In the final version of that law, wines and cider were exempted, and beer wasn't mentioned at all. Of the laws that actually passed, the Watts Bill exempted wines, cider, and fruit brandies sold in large quantities but said nothing about beer.

In 1908 came another statewide vote on prohibition. The debate was hot and heavy. National organizations got involved. "It is well known that the Brewers' Association . . . determined to spend millions in trying to stem the temperance wave in the South," noted Daniel Jay Whitener in *Prohibition in North Carolina: 1715–1945*.[21] This time, the prohibition vote passed. According to Whitener, this meant that "to sell or manufacture any spirituous, vinous, fermented or malt liquors, or intoxicating bitters was made unlawful. Druggists were allowed to sell upon written prescription of a licensed physician for sickness only. Wine and cider made from grapes, berries, or fruits could be manufactured and sold, provided the sale was made at the place of manufacture and in sealed packages of not less than two and one-half gallons. Cider could be sold in any quantity by the manufacturer from fruit grown on his lands."[22]

That law went into effect in January 1909, well before nationwide Prohibition. But it had numerous loopholes. For instance, retail sales were permitted to male "social clubs." In 1923, when Congress passed the Volstead Act, North Carolina passed the Turlington Act to bring its dry laws in line with the national law.

Prohibition lasted until 1933. When it became obvious that national repeal was on the horizon, the North Carolina General Assembly considered several bills to pave the way for the legal sale of alcohol. The one that passed, after much debate, was a beer and wine bill. "By it the sale of beer, lager beer, ale, porter, fruit juices, and light wines containing not more than three and two-tenths per cent of alcohol by weight was legalized," according to Whitener. "To raise revenue, taxes of two dollars per barrel and two cents per bottle were authorized."[23] This went into effect as soon as national Prohibition was lifted.

Post-Prohibition and the Birth of Craft Beer

Although making low-alcohol beer was legal in North Carolina after repeal, brewing did not take off. According to Reino Ojala's *20 Years of American Beers: The '30s & '40s*, no breweries were qualified to operate in North Carolina as of July 1, 1935. However, beer was widely distributed in the state. In 1936, Atlantic Brewing Company (headquartered in Atlanta) began operating a brewing and bottling plant in Charlotte, and beer was once again being made in North Carolina. However, like regional breweries in most of the rest of the country, Atlantic couldn't keep up with national competition from Anheuser-Busch, Pabst, and other brewing giants. It closed its doors in 1956.

Stroh Brewery Company opened a plant in Winston-Salem in 1970 (it closed in 1999), and Miller Brewing Company opened one in Eden in 1978. But aside from those two industry giants, nothing popped up in North Carolina until the 1980s. That shouldn't come as a surprise. At the end of the 1970s, only 44 breweries existed in the entire United States, down from a peak of 3,200 prior to Prohibition.

In 1980, Uli Bennewitz emigrated from Germany to the United States, eventually ending up in Manteo. He missed the rich German lagers he had grown up with and decided to open a German-style combination brewery and restaurant. He faced only one obstacle: it was illegal. Undaunted, Bennewitz lobbied the North Carolina General Assembly. In 1985, a law passed that allowed brewpubs to operate in the state. With that act, Bennewitz changed the future of North Carolina brewing. He opened his brewpub, Weeping Radish, in 1986 in Manteo, where it remained until moving to Grandy in 2006. Bennewitz also opened another brewpub in Durham in 1988; it has since closed.

From 1990 on, North Carolina saw a rush of brewery development, closely following the national trend. The state's industry grew from four breweries in 1990 to 28 by 2000, even through the rash of brewery closings the industry saw nationwide.

The brewing industry in North Carolina received an additional boost after the passing of the Pop the Cap law (HB 392) in 2006, which raised the legal alcohol limit for beer to 14.9 percent ABV. From 28 breweries in 2000, the state was up to 48 by the end of 2010, despite seeing 20 closings in as many years.

Today, the state's brewing industry is thriving. Despite its checkered past, North Carolina has become one of the most notable brewing centers in the southeastern United States.

A Timeline of North Carolina Beer

1770—The town of Cross Creek becomes the site of the state's first documented brewery, though whether or not the brewery was a commercial business is undetermined.

1774—Single Brothers' Brewery and Distillery opens in Salem.

1807—A brewery opens in Wilkinson's Alley in Wilmington.

1813—Single Brothers' Brewery closes.

1822—Thomas Holmes of Salisbury establishes his brewery and advertises in the *Western Carolinian* for supplies of local barley and hops.

1874—The "local option" law is passed. It prohibits "the sale of spirituous liquors in townships where the people so determined."

1881—A general prohibition law "with home-made wines and beer excepted" is passed by the North Carolina General Assembly but is defeated by a popular vote.

1903—The Watts Bill passes. It prohibits "both the sale and the manufacture of liquor outside of incorporated towns."

1905—The Ward Law passes. It prohibits "the manufacturing of liquors in towns of less than 1,000 inhabitants."

1908—An act "to prohibit the manufacture and sale of intoxicating liquors in North Carolina" is passed, making the sale or manufacture of "any spirituous, vinous, fermented, or malt liquors or intoxicating bitters" illegal. The act has many loopholes.

1909—The general prohibition act passed in 1908 goes into effect on January 1. National Prohibition will follow 11 years later.

1920—Prohibition begins when the 18th Amendment goes into effect on January 16.

1933—North Carolina votes against ratification of the 21st Amendment.

The 21st Amendment repeals the 18th Amendment in December, thereby ending Prohibition.

1935—Two years after the federal repeal, North Carolina repeals Prohibition.

1936—The North Carolina Beer and Wine Wholesalers Association is established.

Atlantic Brewing Company, based in Georgia, opens a brewing and bottling branch in Charlotte that becomes the state's first post-Prohibition brewery.

1937—The ABC Commission is established by the North Carolina government. It will go on to form most of the regulatory structure that still exists within the state.

1955—Atlantic Brewing Company becomes the first beer canning operation in North Carolina.

1956—Atlantic Brewing Company shuts its doors. The Charlotte branch is the last of the company's operations to close.

1970—Stroh Brewery Company opens a brewery in Winston-Salem.

1978—Miller Brewing Company opens a brewery in Eden.

1983—The legal drinking age in North Carolina is raised from 18 to 21.

1985—An amendment to North Carolina laws spearheaded by Uli Bennewitz makes brewpubs legal in the state.

1986—On July 4, Uli Bennewitz's Weeping Radish in Manteo becomes North Carolina's first brewpub.

1987—Chesapeake Bay Brewing Company wins a Gold Medal for "Chesbay Double Bock" at the Great American Beer Festival. It is North Carolina's first GABF medal.

1988—Weeping Radish opens a second brewpub in Durham.

Dilworth Brewery opens a brewery and restaurant in Charlotte.

1989—Greenshields Brewing Company brews its first batch at its brewpub in Raleigh.

1990—Loggerhead Brewing opens in Greensboro.

Weeping Radish wins a Silver Medal for its "Hopfen Helles" at the Great American Beer Festival.

1991—Spring Garden Brewing opens in Greensboro on March 12. It will later become Red Oak Brewery.

1992—Cottonwood Brewery opens a brewpub in Boone.

Dilworth Brewery wins a Bronze Medal for its "Albemarle Ale" at the Great American Beer Festival.

1993—Smoky Mountain Brewing Company opens in Waynesville.

1994—Toisnot Brewing opens in Wilson on January 1.

Wilmington Brewery opens in Wilmington.

Olde Hickory Brewery opens in Hickory.

Highland Brewing Company brews its first batch in Asheville at its facility on Biltmore Avenue.

1995—Carolina Brewing Company starts making beer in Holly Springs.

Johnson Beer Company, a packaging brewery, opens in Charlotte.

Loggerhead Brewing closes its facility in Greensboro.

Old Raleigh Brewing opens in Raleigh.

Southend Brewery and Smokehouse opens a brewpub in Charlotte.

Carolina Brewery opens its doors to diners and drinkers in Chapel Hill.

Front Street Brewery brews its first batch in Wilmington.

Cottonwood Brewery wins a Bronze Medal for its "Belgian Amber Framboise" at the Great American Beer Festival.

1996—Huske Hardware House opens a brewpub and begins brewing in Fayetteville.

Pinehurst Village Brewery brews and bottles its first batch in Aberdeen.

Steve & Clark's Brewpub opens its doors in downtown Durham at the old Weeping Radish site on Duke Street.

Tomcat Brewing opens in Raleigh.

Top of the Hill begins brewing at its brewpub right in the middle of downtown Chapel Hill.

Woodhouse Brewing opens in Kernersville.

1997—A year after opening, Woodhouse Brewing closes.

Jack of the Wood opens in downtown Asheville.

Old Raleigh Brewing closes its doors.

Pale Ale Brewery begins operations where Tomcat Brewing ended in Raleigh.

Carolina Beer & Beverage opens in Mooresville in November.

Cottonwood Brewery wins a Bronze Medal for "Low Down Brown" at the Great American Beer Festival.

1998—Cross Creek Brewing opens in Fayetteville.

Dilworth Brewery closes its doors in Charlotte.

Two Moons Brew-N-View opens in Asheville as a movie theater/brewpub.

Southend Brewery and Smokehouse opens in Raleigh in November.

Cottonwood Brewery wins a Silver Medal for "Hortons Irish Stout" at the Great American Beer Festival.

1999—Two Moons Brew-N-View changes its name to Asheville Pizza and Brewing Company.

Rock Creek Brewing moves to North Carolina from Virginia. It takes over the Pale Ale Brewery facility in Raleigh.

Stroh Brewery Company closes its Winston-Salem brewery.

Ham's Restaurant and Brewhouse starts brewing in Greenville in March.

Catawba Valley Brewing Company opens in Glen Alpine in July.

Lake Norman Brewing Company opens in Cornelius in December.

Cottonwood Brewery wins a Bronze Medal for its "Great Pumpkin Spiced Ale" and Wilmington Brewing Company wins a Silver Medal for "Dergy's Amber" at the Great American Beer Festival.

2000—Johnson Beer Company closes its doors in Charlotte.

Williamsville Brewery takes over Wilmington Brewery in Farmville.

Olde Hickory Brewery opens a second microbrewery in Hickory.

Lake Norman Brewing Company closes its Cornelius brewery in June.

In November, Carolina Beer & Beverage takes over the Cottonwood line of beers. Don Richardson, formerly of Cottonwood, assumes lead brewing responsibilities at Carolina Beer & Beverage.

2001—Chesapeake Bay Brewing Company buys the Rock Creek Brewing name and starts making beer at the same location in Raleigh.

Tobacco Roadhouse begins brewing where Steve & Clark's Brewpub left off in Durham.

The Mash House Brewery & Chophouse wins a Gold Medal for its "Hoppy Hour IPA" at the Great American Beer Festival.

French Broad Brewing Co. opens in Asheville. Founder Jonas Rembert left Jack of the Wood to start the new brewery.

2002—Olde Hickory Brewery renames its original brewpub Amos Howard's Restaurant & Brew Works. The microbrewery it opened in 2000 retains the Olde Hickory name.

Liberty Steakhouse brews its first batch in High Point.

Outer Banks Brewing Station wins a Bronze Medal for its "LemonGrass Wheat" at the Great American Beer Festival.

2003—Pop the Cap holds its first official meeting in January.

Chesapeake Bay Brewing Company closes its doors in Raleigh in April.

Edenton Brewing Company opens on the old Chesapeake Bay site in November.

Appalachian Craft Brewery opens its doors in Fletcher.

2004—The Duck-Rabbit Craft Brewery opens in Farmville in March on the site of the now-closed Williamsville Brewery.

Natty Greene's Pub & Brewing Co. opens in Greensboro during the summer.

A fire at the brewpub forces Greenshields Brewing Company to close its doors in August.

Heinzelmännchen opens in Sylva.

Carolina Beer & Beverage wins a Gold Medal for "Charleston Brown" at the World Beer Cup.

Ham's Restaurant and Brewhouse wins a Bronze Medal for "Charlie's Barley Amber Ale" at the Great American Beer Festival.

2005—House Bill 392—the "Pop the Cap" bill—is introduced to the North Carolina House of Representatives on February 24.

Foothills Brewing opens in Winston-Salem in March.

Pisgah Brewing Company starts brewing in Black Mountain in June.

North Carolina's new 14.9 percent ABV cap is born on August 13.

2006—Weeping Radish moves its operation from Manteo to Jarvisburg.

Highland Brewing opens a new, larger brewery in East Asheville. The old brewery on Biltmore Avenue underneath Barley's Taproom is phased out and closed.

Outer Banks Brewing Station wins a Bronze Medal for "Smolder Bock" and Highland Brewing Company wins a Silver Medal for "Black Mocha Stout" at the World Beer Cup.

Duck-Rabbit wins a Bronze Medal for its "Milk Stout," Natty Greene's wins a Silver Medal for "Old Town Brown," Carolina Brewery wins a Gold Medal for "Flagship IPA," and Ham's Restaurant and Brewhouse wins a Gold Medal for "Sunfest Lager" at the Great American Beer Festival, marking the greatest haul of medals North Carolina has seen.

2007—Natty Greene's opens a production-only facility in addition to its brewpub to keep up with demand. The first bottles of Natty Greene's core beers roll off the line in the spring.

Triangle Brewing Company opens a microbrewery in Durham on July 4.

Carolina Brewery opens its second brewpub location in Pittsboro on August 6.

Edenton Brewing Company changes ownership and names. Big Boss Brewing Company resumes brewing operations at the same location in Raleigh.

Craggie Brewing Company opens its doors in Asheville.

Foothills Brewing wins Silver Medals for its "Baltic-Style Porter" and "Gruffmeister Bock" at the Great American Beer Festival.

2008—Wedge Brewing Company opens in Asheville and begins servings its Iron Rail IPA and Community Porter.

Aviator Brewing Company opens and begins brewing in an airport hangar in Fuquay-Varina.

Ham's Restaurant and Brewhouse wins a Bronze Medal for "Peg Leg Pale Ale" and Foothills Brewing wins a Gold Medal for "People's Porter" and a Silver Medal for "Total Eclipse Stout" at the World Beer Cup.

Highland Brewing Company wins a Silver Medal for its "Black Mocha Stout" at the Great American Beer Festival.

2009—LoneRider Brewing Company makes its official debut on January 20 and offers its first brewery tour three days later.

Boylan Bridge Brewpub opens in Raleigh on February 27. Its first beers are "Gateway Golden," "Rail Pale Ale," "Bruno Bitter," "Polar Bear Winter Warmer," "Pullman Porter," and "Southbound Stout."

OysterHouse Brewing Company begins brewing operations at the Lobster Trap in Asheville.

Olde Mecklenburg Brewery starts production in Charlotte.

Lexington Avenue Brewing Co. opens in Asheville.

Nantahala Brewing Company opens in Bryson City.

Railhouse Brewery opens in Aberdeen.

Four Friends Brewing opens in Charlotte.

Foothills Brewing wins a Bronze Medal for "Sexual Chocolate Imperial Stout" and The Duck-Rabbit Craft Brewery wins a Gold Medal for "Baltic-Style Porter" and a Bronze Medal for "Barrel-Aged Baltic-Style Porter" at the Great American Beer Festival.

2010—Appalachian Craft Brewery moves and changes its name to Southern Appalachian Brewery.

Loe's Brewing Company opens in Hickory.

Natty Greene's opens its Raleigh location in the Powerhouse Building.

Roth Brewing Company, the state's first nanobrewery, opens on July 16.

Fullsteam opens its doors on the anniversary of the passage of Pop the Cap.

Green Man Brewery is bought by Jack of the Wood and begins brewing under new ownership.

Carolina Beer & Beverage sells Carolina Brands, Cottonwood Brands, and its brewhouse to Foothills Brewing. Foothills begins construction on a new production facility.

Outer Banks Brewing Station wins a Silver Medal for its "LemonGrass Wheat," Olde Hickory Brewery wins a Silver Medal for "Irish Walker," Foothills wins a Silver Medal for "Sexual Chocolate Imperial Stout," and Duck-Rabbit wins a Gold Medal for "Milk Stout" at the World Beer Cup.

LoneRider Brewing Company wins a Gold Medal for "Sweet Josie Brown" and Foothills Brewing wins a Gold Medal for "Bourbon Barrel Aged Sexual Chocolate Imperial Stout" and a Bronze Medal for "Foothills Oktoberfest" at the Great American Beer Festival.

2011—Ass Clown Brewing Company begins brewing in Cornelius in April.

Lumina Winery & Brewery begins producing beer in Wilmington.

In June, Bull City Burger and Brewery opens in Durham, becoming the city's first brewpub.

NoDa Brewing Company opens in Charlotte in October.

Frog Level Brewing Company brews its first beer in Waynesville in October.

Full Moon Café & Brewery adds a brewery to its operation in Manteo.

Lexington Avenue Brewery wins a Silver Medal for its "Porter," LoneRider wins a Silver Medal for "Deadeye Jack," and Foothills wins a Silver Medal for "2010 Bourbon Barrel Aged Sexual Chocolate Imperial Stout" at the Great American Beer Festival.

Notes

[1] Christoph von Graffenried, *Christoph von Graffenried's Account of the Founding of New Bern,* ed. and trans. Vincent H. Todd and Julius Goebel (1920; online edition, Documenting the American South, University Library, UNC–Chapel Hill, 2003), http://docsouth.unc.edu/nc/graffenried/graffenried.html (accessed November 7, 2011), 319.

[2] John Brickell, *The Natural History of North Carolina* (Dublin: James Carson, 1737), http://www.archive.org/details/naturalhistoryof00bric (accessed November 8, 2011), 38.

[3] Ibid. 39.

[4] Claude Joseph Sauthier, *Plan of the Town of Crosscreek in Cumberland County, North Carolina* (map, 1770, North Carolina State Archives, Raleigh).

5 James D. Kornwolf and Georgiana Wallis Kornwolf, *Architecture and Town Planning in Colonial North America* (Baltimore: Johns Hopkins University Press, 2002), 462.

6 Stanley Baron, *Brewed in America: A History of Beer and Ale in the United States* (Boston: Little, Brown, 1962), 50.

7 Chowan County, Ordinary Bonds and Records, 1739–1867, North Carolina State Archives, Raleigh.

8 William Lenoir's distilling book, Folder 289, Lenoir Family Papers #00426, Southern Historical Collection, Louis Round Wilson Special Collections Library, UNC–Chapel Hill.

9 Henry Gunnisson, "Brewery," *Wilmington Gazette* (Wilmington, NC), May 12, 1807, http://ncecho.cdmhost.com/cdm/ref/collection/p15016coll1/id/23203 (accessed November 8, 2011).

10 Thomas Holmes, "Beer and Porter House," *Western Carolinian* (Salisbury, NC), April 1, 1823, http://ncecho.cdmhost.com/u?/p15016coll1,18025 (accessed November 8, 2011).

11 Thomas Holmes, "Hops," *Western Carolinian* (Salisbury, NC), June 10, 1823, http://ncecho.cdmhost.com/cdm/ref/collection/p15016coll1/id/18057 (accessed November 8, 2011).

12 Thomas Holmes, "House of Entertainment," *Western Carolinian* (Salisbury, NC), May 8, 1827, http://ncecho.cdmhost.com/u?/p15016coll1,18998 (accessed November 8, 2011).

13 "Domestic Beer, Porter, &c.," *Western Carolinian* (Salisbury, NC), August 19, 1828, http://ncecho.cdmhost.com/u?/p15016coll1,19327 (accessed November 8, 2011).

14 Ibid.

[15] "Recipe for making Chinese Beer," *Carolina Watchman* (Salisbury, NC), July 22, 1847, http://ncecho.cdmhost.com/u?/p15016coll1,1068 (accessed November 8, 2011).

[16] "A Remedy Proposed," *Carolina Watchman* (Salisbury, NC), June 20, 1850, http://ncecho.cdmhost.com/u?/p15016coll1,1784 (accessed November 8, 2011).

[17] Confederate States of America, *Tariff of the Confederate States of America* (1861; online edition, Documenting the American South, University Library, UNC–Chapel Hill, 1999), http://docsouth.unc.edu/imls/tariff/tariff.html (accessed November 8, 2011), 5.

[18] James M. Matthews, ed., *The Statutes at Large of the Confederate States of America, Passed at the Fourth Session of the First Congress, 1863–64* (1864; online edition, Documenting the American South. University Library, UNC–Chapel Hill, 2001), http://docsouth.unc.edu/imls/23conf/23conf.html (accessed November 8, 2011), 179.

[19] Francis Peyre Porcher, *Resources of the Southern Fields and Forests* (1863; online edition, Documenting the American South. University Library, UNC–Chapel Hill, 2001), http://docsouth.unc.edu/imls/porcher/porcher.html (accessed November 8, 2011), 279–80.

[20] Daniel Jay Whitener, *Prohibition in North Carolina, 1715–1945* (Chapel Hill: University of North Carolina Press, 1946), 50.

[21] Ibid., 166.

[22] Ibid., 162.

[23] Ibid., 199.

How Beer is Made

Ingredients

All beer is made from five essential ingredients.

Water is the most important ingredient in beer. Beer is mostly water, so it is essential to have clean water that tastes good in order to make good beer. Many of the world's classic beer styles have evolved because of good local water profiles—the balance of minerals and salts naturally dissolved into the water that give it a hard or soft character, as well as a distinctive flavor.

North Carolina typically has good, neutral, relatively soft water that makes excellent beer.

Malted barley is the source of most of the sugar in beer. Barley is a grain commonly grown throughout the world but especially in northern Europe, the American Midwest, Canada, and Australia. Unlike other cereal grains, it is high in starch and low in protein and has a fibrous husk. All of these characteristics make it ideal for use in making beer.

When barley is harvested, it is not immediately ready for beer production. It must first be *malted*. Malting is a process in which the grain is soaked in water, which causes germination of the seed to start. Natural enzymes in the barley then begin to change the starch already present in the kernel into sugar. Other enzymes break down cell walls in the barley, making the hard, pebble-like barley kernel soft and sugary. The maltster then applies heat, arresting the germination process and caramelizing the sugar in the kernel.

Maltsters use many different types of heating and roasting techniques to make different colors and flavors of malt, ranging from extremely light pilsner malt, used as a base malt in the lightest beers, to deep black roasted malt, which can impart an espresso-like character and color to a beer. A vast array of caramel and toasted malts lies in between. Brewers can choose from well over 200 different types of malts from different maltsters and suppliers. All impart different flavors, colors, and even textures to beer.

Hops are the flowers and fruiting bodies of the plant *Humulus lupulus*. They have bright green flowers resembling pine cones growing in bunches from perennial bines 20 to 30 feet tall. Brewers use hops to add bitterness to beer to counteract the sweetness of the malt. The hundreds of different types of cultivated hops provide their own flavors to beer. The flavors can range from citrusy and pine-like to grassy, earthy, or leathery, and even to apple, pear, blueberry, or other fruit flavors.

Hops weren't always used in beer. Throughout history, many other herbs have been put into beer to counteract sweetness, among them sweet gale, yarrow, spruce, pine, heather, bee balm, and even some fairly dangerous ingredients like wormwood and witch hazel. Over time, hops were adopted not only for their pleasant flavor but because they are a natural antibacterial agent. Their presence in brewing has significantly increased the shelf life of beer.

Yeast is unique as an ingredient in brewing because it is actually a living organism. For thousands of years, brewers merely made liquids they knew would eventually turn into beer, then left them out for the apparently spontaneous reaction that would sooner or later occur. They knew that if they added some of the beer from previous batches, or even bread made from a previous batch of beer, that the reaction would happen more quickly. It wasn't until Louis Pasteur's groundbreaking work in the mid-19th century that people understood that live organisms in the liquid were eating the sugar-rich solution and excreting carbon dioxide and ethanol—two of the components that make beer most pleasant to drinkers—as well as up to 900 other chemicals that add flavor.

Brewers use two major families of yeast: ale yeast and lager yeast. These are often incorrectly referred to as "top fermenting" yeast (ale yeast) and "bottom fermenting" yeast (lager yeast) because of how brewers used to harvest the yeast before the advent of modern technology. In reality, fermentation takes place throughout the solution. The primary difference between ale yeast and lager yeast is the temperature at which they best ferment. Ale yeast ferments around room temperature, from

60 degrees to 75 degrees Fahrenheit, whereas lager yeast ferments best between 45 degrees and 60 degrees. Ale yeast also tends to have a much more robust *ester* profile, evoking a wide range of fruit flavors, while lager yeast creates much more neutral, crisp, clean beers.

Literally thousands of yeasts from these two families are used around the world to make beer.

Adjuncts often get a bad rap. Adjuncts are sources of sugar used for brewing that are not malted barley. When people speak of adjuncts in brewing, they are typically referring to a macrobrewery's use of corn and rice in light American lagers, primarily to add more fermentable sugar to the beer without adding any flavor or character.

However, adjuncts can also be used to add an enormous amount of flavor to beer. Any non-barley grain is considered an adjunct. Rye, wheat, oats, buckwheat, spelt, and sorghum are all used as adjuncts, and all impart their own flavor. Adjuncts can also refer to sugar additions like turbinado, demerara, brown sugar, molasses, agave syrup, candi sugar, honey, and maple syrup. Finally, many clever brewers use a wide range of fruits and vegetables as sources of starch and sugar as well. These include sweet potatoes, pumpkins, and squash. Anything with natural starch or sugar can be used as an adjunct in beer.

The Brewing Process

Milling

When a brewer starts a batch of beer, the first thing he does is mill the barley. Barley usually comes to a brewery in whole-kernel form. Those kernels must be crushed to expose the insides to water more efficiently in the later steps. Brewers only crush grain. They do not mill it to a flour. They want to leave the husks of the barley intact to use as a natural filter later in the process.

Mashing

Once the grain is milled, the brewer adds heated water. The heat and water reactivate the enzymes that were at work in the barley during germination, which restarts the conversion of starches into sugars.

Since water is an excellent solvent, it also acts as a base for the sugars to dissolve into, meaning that the sugars can easily be extracted from the grain.

Lautering

Lautering is the process of removing the liquid—now considered *wort*—from the grain. The wort is drained through the grain itself, the husks from the barley acting as a natural filter bed. While this is happening, clean hot water is sprayed over the top of the grain bed in a process called *sparging*. Sparging rinses the remaining sugar from the grain bed, allowing the brewer to use as much as possible of the sugar that was originally present in the barley.

Boiling

The wort is then transferred to a kettle and boiled. Boiling serves several important functions in brewing. It sterilizes the wort, ensuring that no bacteria or wild yeasts are present. It drives off volatile sulfuric compounds naturally found in barley that can lend an unpleasant egg or cabbage flavor and aroma in beer. Boiling allows for the formation of certain calcium compounds that help protein precipitate from the solution to create clearer beer. Finally, boiling is when brewers add the majority of the hops—and sometimes other ingredients—to the beer.

Brewers are very careful about when hops are added to the boil. The longer hops are in contact with the boiling wort, the more bitterness is derived from the hops, and the less aroma and flavor. Because of this, brewers normally use a *hop schedule* that specifies the amount of hops to be added at the beginning or middle of the boil for bitterness, and the amount to be added near the end of the boil for flavor and aroma. Since aroma compounds are delicate and can easily be boiled off, any ingredients the brewer wishes to retain the aroma of are normally added right at the end of the boil.

Fermentation and Conditioning

Boiling normally takes an hour at minimum. Afterward, the wort is chilled to fermentation temperature, and yeast is added. It is at this point that the liquid actually becomes beer. Yeast can finish fermenting in as little as three days to as many as 30 days, depending on the strain of the yeast, the amount of sugar in the solution, and the temperature of fermentation. Brewers often allow the beer to sit through a period of cold conditioning after fermentation is complete.

Packaging and Distribution

After the fermenting and conditioning are completed, the beer is carbonated and packaged. In North Carolina, every major type of packaging is employed: kegs of all sizes, bottles, cans, and growlers (half-gallon jugs). Once the beer has been packaged, it is on its way to consumers for their enjoyment.

Brewpubs & Breweries

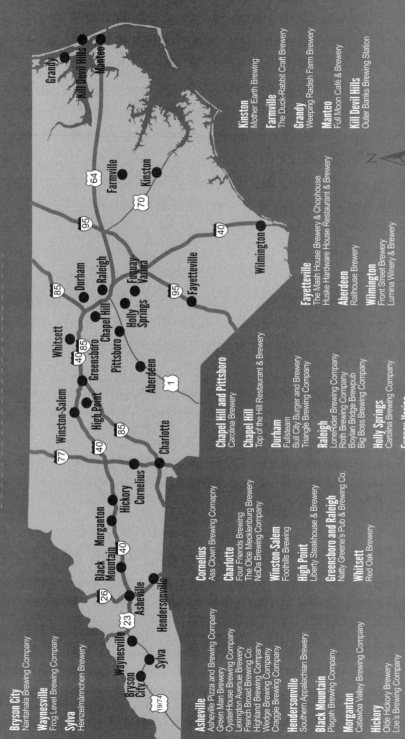

Bryson City
Nantahala Brewing Company

Waynesville
Frog Level Brewing Company

Sylva
Heinzelmännchen Brewery

Asheville
Asheville Pizza and Brewing Company
Green Man Brewery
OysterHouse Brewing Company
Lexington Avenue Brewery
French Broad Brewing Co.
Highland Brewing Company
Wedge Brewing Company
Craggie Brewing Company

Hendersonville
Southern Appalachian Brewery

Black Mountain
Pisgah Brewing Company

Morganton
Catawba Valley Brewing Company

Hickory
Olde Hickory Brewery
Loe's Brewing Company

Cornelius
Ass Clown Brewing Comapny

Charlotte
Four Friends Brewing
The Olde Mecklenburg Brewery
NoDa Brewing Company

Winston-Salem
Foothills Brewing

High Point
Liberty Steakhouse & Brewery

Greensboro and Raleigh
Natty Greene's Pub & Brewing Co.

Whitsett
Red Oak Brewery

Chapel Hill and Pittsboro
Carolina Brewery

Chapel Hill
Top of the Hill Restaurant & Brewery

Durham
Fullsteam
Bull City Burger and Brewery
Triangle Brewing Company

Raleigh
LoneRider Brewing Company
Roth Brewing Company
Boylan Bridge Brewpub
Big Boss Brewing Company

Holly Springs
Carolina Brewing Company

Fuquay-Varina
Aviator Brewing Company

Fayetteville
The Mash House Brewery & Chophouse
Huske Hardware House Restaurant & Brewery

Aberdeen
Railhouse Brewery

Wilmington
Front Street Brewery
Lumina Winery & Brewery

Kinston
Mother Earth Brewing

Farmville
The Duck-Rabbit Craft Brewery

Grandy
Weeping Radish Farm Brewery

Manteo
Full Moon Café & Brewery

Kill Devil Hills
Outer Banks Brewing Station

A Primer on Beer Styles

Beer styles are in a constant state of flux. Most of the familiar styles have grown out of brewing tradition over the past few hundred years. And as with art, more new styles—often new takes on traditional styles—are being invented every day.

Style guidelines are used for judging beers in competitions, both at the amateur and professional levels. More importantly, style definitions allow consumers to know what to expect when they pick a beer off a shelf or order something in a bar.

Most beer falls into two basic categories: ales and lagers. This refers to the type of yeast used in brewing. All ales are brewed with *Saccharomyces cerevisiae*. Hundreds, if not thousands, of strains of *S. cerevisiae* are used around the world in brewing and baking—even in the bread yeast customers buy at the store. All lagers are brewed with *Saccharomyces pastorianus*. Two major strains of *S. pastorianus* are used in brewing worldwide. Some brewers use wild yeasts or other controlled yeasts such as *Brettanomyces bruxellensis* or *Brettanomyces lambicus* and even bacteria such as *lactobacillus*, *pediococcus*, or *acetobacter* for different flavors in fermentation.

Ale yeast and lager yeast were once misidentified as, respectively "top fermenting" and "bottom fermenting" because of the methods brewers used to harvest the yeast. It is now known that fermentation takes place throughout beer and that, eventually, all yeast settles to the bottom and can be collected by brewers. However, the terms are still in frequent use.

The following is not a complete list of beer styles, but one that attempts to highlight most of the styles available in North Carolina. Many of the beers brewed in North Carolina defy conventional style guides and are well worth seeking out. For more information, check out the Beer Judge Certification Program (bjcp.org/stylecenter.php) and the Brewers Association Beer Style Guidelines (brewersassociation.org/pages/publications/beer-style-guidelines).

Lagers

Lager literally means "to store." This is in reference to the origin of many lager beers, which were stored in caves during warm summer months to complete fermentation. In the 1800s, brewing scientists discovered that the yeast in lagers was actually a different type than was used in ales. It ferments at a lower temperature for a longer period of time. Lager yeast has few esters (the fruity flavors normally present in ales) and often has a lingering light sulfuric flavor, giving lagers their characteristic dryness and crispness.

In 2011, scientists discovered a yeast called *Saccharomyces eubayanas* in Patagonia that is thought to be the parent organism of lager yeast.

Premium American Lager. The most common beer in the world. Very pale. Highly carbonated. Not malty or hoppy. High use of adjuncts such as corn and rice lighten the body of the beer. Commercial examples: Budweiser, Miller Genuine Draft. No craft examples in North Carolina.

Lite American Lager. A "light" version of premium American lager with less residual sugar, less alcohol, and less flavor. Commercial examples: Bud Light, Coors Light. No craft examples in North Carolina.

Munich Helles. Sweet, malty, crisp golden lager brewed using traditional German noble hops, which lend a light, spicy, floral aroma. North Carolina examples: Olde Mecklenburg Mecklenburger, Red Oak Hummin' Bird.

Bohemian Pilsner. Light, grainy, malty, and complex. Traditionally brewed using Saaz hops, which lend a light bitterness and a spicy and floral character. North Carolina examples: Aviator Crazy Pils, Foothills Torch Pilsner.

German Pilsner. Traditionally, a German copy of Bohemian pilsner. Generally drier and crisper than Bohemian pilsner, brewed using other traditional German hops and having slightly higher carbonation. North Carolina examples: Olde Mecklenburg Captain James Jack Pilsner, Weeping Radish Corolla Gold.

Vienna Lager. A rich, malty amber lager. No hop aroma or flavor. Even though this beer has a sweet flavor, it finishes crisp and dry. North Carolina example: Red Oak Amber Lager.

Marzen/Oktoberfest. Traditionally, a version of Vienna lager brewed in Munich, this beer is now associated primarily with the annual Oktoberfest festival there. North Carolina examples: Foothills Oktoberfest, Highland Clawhammer Oktoberfest.

Munich Dunkel. *Dunkel* means "dark" in German. A dark, rich, malty lager that often has notes of chocolate, caramel, coffee, or toast. Based on traditional Marzen but darker, more complex, and higher in alcohol. North Carolina examples: Mother Earth Dark Cloud Munich Dunkel, Olde Mecklenburg Dunkel Lager.

Schwarzbier. Literally "black beer." Similar to a Munich dunkel but not normally as sweet and rich. Flavors tend toward roasted or coffee bitterness and moderate hop bitterness. Sometimes referred to as a "black pilsner." North Carolina examples: Duck-Rabbit Schwarzbier, Weeping Radish Black Radish.

Bock. A dark, strong, toasty, malty lager that originated in the northern German city of Einbeck. *Bock* is a corruption of *Einbeck* in the Bavarian dialect. Since *bock* means "goat" in German, goats are often used in advertising. Bocks sometimes have flavors reminiscent of dark or dried fruits. North Carolina examples: Olde Mecklenburg Frueh Bock, Bull City "Goat" Bullock Bock.

Maibock/Helles Bock. A paler version of traditional bock. Sometimes drier or more hoppy, often with rich, malty complexity but none of the dark fruit flavors. *Helles* means "pale" and *Mai* means "May," referring to the fact that Maibock is traditionally served in the springtime. North Carolina examples: Foothills Gruffmeister Maibock, Carolina Brewing Company Carolina Spring Bock.

Doppelbock. A richer, more alcoholic version of a bock, sometimes with notes of caramel or chocolate in addition to rich fruitiness. *Doppel* means "double." Doppelbocks are normally much sweeter and stronger than traditional bocks. Most are dark, but occasional versions are pale. North Carolina examples: Duck-Rabbit Doppelbock, Olde Hickory Doppelbock.

Baltic Porter. A version of traditional English porter originating from countries around the Baltic Sea. Similar to English porters in its coffee, chocolate, and caramel notes, but sweeter and more alcoholic, with notes of molasses and dark fruit. North Carolina example: Duck-Rabbit Baltic Porter.

Ales

The one trait all ales have in common is that they are made with some strain of ale yeast. Ale yeasts ferment quickly and close to room temperature. Their notable flavor characteristics come from esters, which can contribute a wide range of fruit flavors, and fusel alcohols, which contribute flavors reminiscent of port or sherry. Ale yeast is one of the most common organisms in the world and was the first organism to have its genome mapped.

Bitter, Best Bitter, Extra Special Bitter. These are British pale ales. They generally have a rich, malty body, often with caramel or toffee notes, and a notable hop presence. Bitter (or standard/ordinary bitter) is the mildest version. A slightly stronger, hoppier version would be called special bitter, best bitter, or premium bitter. Stronger and hoppier yet is extra special bitter or strong bitter. North Carolina examples: Foothills Rainbow Trout ESB, Boylan Bridge Bruno Bitter.

Mild English Brown Ale. The word *mild* originally referred to a beer that was young or fresh. Now, it refers to a light brown ale with moderate hop bitterness. There are two varieties of English brown ale. Southern English brown is sweet, malty, and nutty and has notes of chocolate and dark fruit. Northern English brown is drier and hoppier. North Carolina examples: Big Boss Bad Penny, Natty Greene's Old Town Brown.

American Brown Ale. Similar to English brown ale—sweet, malty, nutty, and chocolaty—but with a much larger hop profile. American brown normally uses citrusy American hops. North Carolina examples: LoneRider Sweet Josie Brown, Duck-Rabbit Brown Ale, Carolina Brewing Company Carolina Nut Brown Ale.

Brown Porter. Porters are, essentially, dark brown ales. Brewers tend to use "black" or "black patent" malt to flavor porters, giving them a distinctive coffee/espresso note, along with chocolate, malt, and nutty notes. Brown porters are the lighter and sweeter of the two porters and in some cases may not be easily distinguished from brown ales but for the inclusion of black malt. North Carolina examples: Mash House Brown Porter, Boylan Bridge Pullman Porter.

Robust Porter. Robust porters are darker, roastier, more alcoholic versions of brown porters. They have a definite coffee/espresso note from the inclusion of black malt and can also have notes of dark chocolate or burnt caramel. North Carolina examples: Foothills People's Porter, Duck-Rabbit Porter, LoneRider Deadeye Jack Porter.

Scottish Ales. A wide range of Scottish ales exists, but few make their way into the American market. Malty ales with almost no hop character, they can range from very light and fairly dry to rich, dark, and sweet. They sometimes exhibit a light smoky character but rarely contain peated or peat-smoked malt (the type made for use in Scotch whiskey). Scottish ales are traditionally named in shilling amounts, the lightest being a 60 Shilling (alternately written as "60/-"). Also available are 70 Shilling (70/-), 80 Shilling (80/-), and versions that are gradually darker, sweeter, roastier, smokier, and more alcoholic. North Carolina examples: Highland Tasgall Ale, Bull City Bonnie Brae 60 Shilling Scottish Ale.

Wee Heavies. The darkest and heaviest of Scottish ales. The Scottish version of barleywine, they are sweet , rich, malty, and nutty, with notes of caramel and smoky roastiness. North Carolina examples: Duck-Rabbit Wee Heavy, Huske Hardware Filthy Kilt Wee Heavy, French Broad Wee Heavy-er Scotch Ale.

Irish Red Ale. Similar to Scottish ale, but often drier with more caramel or toffee character. It is named, of course, for the reddish hue it gains from the addition of roasted (but not malted) barley. North Carolina examples: Highland Gaelic Ale, Aviator Hotrod Red.

American Pale Ale. The American version of a British pale ale. Malty with a light sweetness. But American pale ale (like anything with *American* in the name) is really about hops. The least bitter showcase for American hops, it normally exhibits notes of citrus, grass, or pine, depending on the type of hops used. It can have a slight lingering bitter finish. North Carolina examples: Natty Greene's Southern Pale Ale, LoneRider Peacemaker Pale Ale, Carolina Brewing Company Carolina Pale Ale.

Dry Stout. Dry and bitter, with notes of coffee, espresso, and cocoa. Creamy and jet-black with a tan- or brown-colored head. North Carolina examples: Carolina Brewery Old North State Stout, Heinzelmännchen Black Forest Stout.

Sweet Stout/Milk Stout. Sweet stouts, or milk stouts, are made using lactose. Lactose is not fermentable by yeast, so the beers are left with much more residual sweetness. They often exhibit chocolate, coffee, or espresso flavors; the end products can taste like sweetened coffee or, because lactose often has a milky tang, like a chocolate bar. North Carolina example: Duck-Rabbit Milk Stout.

Foreign Extra Stout. Foreign extra stouts are traditionally brewed for tropical markets. They are higher in alcohol than dry or sweet stouts and often exhibit a rather fruity characteristic, as well as the traditional coffee, chocolate, burnt, or roasty notes typical of stouts. North Carolina example: Roth Dark Construct.

American Stout. Like other American style versions, this is high in hops. Because this stout is bitter, the tannic character of the malt tends to stand out, giving the beer notes of bittersweet or baker's chocolate, or even a bitter coffee note. American hops lend a grassy, citrusy, or piney flavor. North Carolina examples: Foothills Total Eclipse Stout, Highland Black Mocha Stout.

Russian Imperial Stout. Big, complex Russian imperial stouts are often favorites in the craft beer market. They are high in alcohol and tend to have big, rich palates full of chocolate, coffee, molasses, caramel, and toffee, as well as dark fruit flavors like plums, raisins, prunes, or dates. They are intense beers. North Carolina examples: Duck-Rabbit Rabid Duck Russian Imperial Stout, Natty Greene's Black Powder Imperial Stout.

English IPA. India pale ales (IPA) are highly hopped pale ales. By the 1760s, English brewers were advised to add extra hops to beer for export to warm climes. By the early 1800s, "pale ale prepared for the Indian market"—soon to be referred to as "India pale ale"—was on sale in England. English IPAs aren't as bitter as their American cousins. While they exhibit the same lightly, sweet, caramel palate, they are traditionally made with British hops, which provide an earthy, floral, and sometimes even leathery flavor. North Carolina examples: Highland Kashmir IPA, Carolina Brewery Flagship IPA.

American IPA. American IPAs are filled with American hops. While a sweet, malty body exists, it is mainly there to support the hops. American hops are more bitter than many other hops and have flavors reminiscent of citrus, pine, or hemp. These beers tend to have a lingering, bitter finish. North Carolina examples: Big Boss High Roller, Foothills Hoppyum IPA, Mother Earth Sisters of the Moon IPA.

Imperial/Double IPA. A big, bold, alcoholic IPA with tons of hops. This beer often resembles a barleywine in strength and character, with rich caramel flavors dominating, but it is really a showcase for hops. It can exhibit citrus, pine, grassy, earthy, floral, herbal, or hemp tones. Some examples even have a note of sulfur to them, which dries out the ultra-sweet body and adds another layer of flavor complexity. North Carolina examples: Foothills Seeing Double IPA, Natty Greene's Cannonball Double IPA.

Black IPA. An IPA made with a slight addition of roasted malt for an extra layer of complexity. The added malt is generally either malted wheat or dehusked barley, to avoid a harsh tannic bitterness. The majority of the bitterness in a black IPA is derived from the hops. The added bitterness can lend a bitter cocoa flavor to the IPA. Versions made with American hops are reminiscent of a chocolate orange. North Carolina examples: LoneRider Grave Robber Black IPA, Olde Hickory Black Raven IPA.

English Barleywine. Barleywine gets its name from its strength, which is often nearly as high as that of wine. It's a strong, rich, malty beer with notes of caramel, toffee, or molasses. It can exhibit bread, nut, and fruit characteristics. English versions are made with mild English hops, which often lend a leathery or woody character to a barleywine. Many barleywines are now vintage-dated and can be aged. Their flavor can change significantly in the bottle over the course of a couple of years. North Carolina examples: Duck-Rabbit Barleywine, Olde Hickory Irish Walker.

American Barleywine. American barleywines, like their English cousins, are sweet, malty, and strong. However, like every other style labeled "American," they have a much higher hop content and a much more bitter character. Because of the sweet backbone of these beers, American barleywines often become a showcase for American hops. They can be very citrusy or piney without being overpoweringly bitter. North Carolina examples: Roth FoeHammer Barleywine, Carolina Brewery Old Familiar Barley Wine.

Weizen/Weissbier. The words *weizen* ("wheat"), *weissbier* ("white beer"), and *hefeweizen* ("yeast wheat") refer to light German beers that are made with high proportions of wheat and very few hops. Wheat lends a full, creamy feel to the beers. Since these beers are often served young, with yeast still in suspension, they often have a light, bready quality. The yeast used in most weissbiers also provides a blend of flavors reminiscent of bananas and cloves—a unique flavor profile. North Carolina examples: LoneRider Shotgun Betty Hefeweizen, Mother Earth Sunny Haze Hefeweizen.

Dunkelweizen. *Dunkelweizen* means "dark wheat." This is exactly what it sounds like: a wheat beer made with dark malts to create a dark beer with a complex palate. The wheat still provides a full, rich feel, but the result is often much more reminiscent of rich malts, caramels, and at times even chocolate. These beers can have a wide range of flavors, from bananas like their "white" brethren to cloves, bubblegum, or vanilla. North Carolina example: Big Boss Dicer.

Witbier. A witbier is a light, wheat-based ale like a weissbier, traditionally made with additions of coriander and bitter (Curaçao) orange peel. Light and zesty, it has a citrus character from the spice additions and the same milky cloudiness and hazy character of other wheat beers. North Carolina examples: Big Boss Blanco Diablo, Mother Earth Weeping Willow Wit, Natty Greene's Wildflower Witbier.

Saison/Biere de Garde. A saison is traditionally a farmhouse ale brewed for workers in the fields. The original versions were low in alcohol and used leftover farm grains—rye, oats, spelt, buckwheat, or whatever else was around. Today's versions are much higher in alcohol and typically use mostly barley. They have a distinctive yeast that produces dry, spicy beer. Some versions have added spices ranging from star anise, cloves, and black pepper to rosemary, thyme, sage, and basil. The color can range from bright yellow to orange. Most versions are highly carbonated. North Carolina examples: Aviator Saison de Aviator, Fullsteam Summer Basil.

Abbey Ale. Abbey ales refer to a range of complex, dry Belgian beers that have traditionally been produced in Trappist monasteries. But only beers produced in eight specific abbeys in Belgium and the Netherlands are allowed to be called "Trappist ales." Although two main styles are recognized—dubbel and tripel—many Belgian- and abbey-style ales defy categorization. Dubbels are dark, dry, malty beers with vinous notes of dark fruit and chocolate. Tripels are high-alcohol golden beers with rich, malty palates and fruity notes. Belgian and abbey ales tend to be quite dry, "digestible," and highly carbonated. North Carolina examples: Highland Seven Sisters Abbey-Style Dubbel, Craggie Dubbelicious, Mother Earth Tripel Overhead, Aviator Devils Tramping Ground Tripel.

Hybrid Styles

Hybrid in this case refers to beers that tend to cross the border between ales and lagers in terms of process. They do not actually use hybrid yeasts, but rather ale yeasts fermented at colder temperatures (as lagers would) or lager yeasts fermented at higher temperatures (as ales would).

Kölsch-Style Beer. A Kölsch is light, clean, and crisp. It is similar to a pilsner, but Kölsch is fermented with clean ale yeasts at low temperatures. Kölsch beers tend to have a light, malty sweetness and a clean, grainy quality. Unlike pilsners, they tend to have a light fruitiness and only a light hop bitterness. Technically, only beer brewed in and around Köln, Germany, is allowed to be called Kölsch. North Carolina examples: Mother Earth Endless River Kölsch, Big Boss Angry Angel, Weeping Radish OBX Kölsch.

California Common/Steam Beer. "California common" beers or "steam" beers refer to a certain type of amber lager made with a lager yeast fermented at higher temperatures like an ale. The style originated in San Francisco prior to refrigeration, when brewers attempted to make traditional lagers in the naturally cool climate of the Bay Area. The beer is fruity and malty, with notes of grain, caramel, and—because of the lager yeast—a bit of sulfur, which dries it out and allows the hops to shine through. The name *Steam Beer* is trademarked by Anchor Brewery in San Francisco, so the style is generally referred to as *California common*. North Carolina examples: Fullsteam Southern Lager, Aviator Steamhead.

Other Styles

The following are unique in that they are variations, rather than strict styles. Fruits or spices can be added to any beer, and anything can be put into a barrel (though brewers might not want to).

Fruit Beer. Simply put, this is beer made with fruit. Berries—raspberries, blueberries, strawberries, blackberries, etc.—tend to be the most popular additions. Wheat beers are one of the most popular bases for fruit beers. In North Carolina, beer/fruit combinations run the gamut from the lightest of pilsners to the darkest of stouts, employing everything from common fruits to really strange ones. For a long time, fruit beers were seen as "starter" beers or "easy" beers. But in the right brewer's hands, these are delicious concoctions full of rich complexity that all beer drinkers should be eager to try. North Carolina examples: Fullsteam First Frost (abbey-style dubbel made with persimmons), Roth Mi Mei Honey Plum Hefeweizen, Liberty Blackberry Wheat (blackberry hefeweizen), Big Boss Big Operator (black ale made with raspberries).

Spice Beer. Beer made with spices—it seems simple but is actually quite complex. Hundreds of different spices can be used in beer. Anything in the kitchen—including rosemary, basil, black pepper, sage, saffron, allspice, vanilla, and ginger, to only name a few—can fall into a brewer's kettle, with amazing results. *Spice beer* also refers to beers made with coffee or chocolate. North Carolina examples: Big Boss Harvest Time (made with pumpkin pie spice), Roth Forgotten Hollow Cinnamon Porter, Outer Banks LemonGrass Wheat Ale, Craggie Antebellum Ale (made with molasses, ginger, and spruce tips).

Smoked Beer. In these beers, a portion of the grain has been smoked, much as traditional North Carolina barbecue is smoked. They can range from the slightly smoky to the intensely smoky, which can taste a little like drinking a smoked sausage. Some brewers smoke their own grain, but most buy grain presmoked. North Carolina examples: Fullsteam Hogwash Hickory-Smoked Porter, Natty Greene's Smoky Mountain Porter.

Barrel-Aged Beer. Barrel-aged beers are stored in barrels after fermentation to pick up flavor from the barrels or, most often, to pick up flavor from what used to be in them. North Carolina has a rich history of bourbon distilleries and is home to a wide range of bourbon-barrel-aged beers. Often, brewers will barrel-age a portion of a batch of beer. Other breweries make beer specifically to be aged in barrels. North Carolina examples: Olde Rabbit's Foot (an imperial stout made as a collaboration among Olde Hickory, Duck-Rabbit, and Foothills, aged in Pappy Van Winkle barrels), Mother Earth Tripel Overhead (Bourbon Barrel Aged).

Sour Beers. The two basic types of sour beers are those that are soured prior to fermentation (via sour mash or flavor additions) and those that are soured after fermentation (via spontaneous fermentation or controlled fermentation using yeast/bacterial blends). Sour mash beers are typically high in lactic acid, which can provide a refreshing, lemony tang. In high concentrations, these beers can have notes that resemble yogurt or sour milk but—amazingly—are quite delicious. Spontaneously fermented beers and those fermented using souring blends are complex, dry beers. Their wide range of flavors runs from vinegar (acetic acid), lemon, apple cider, and tropical fruits to more "funky" flavors sometimes described as "hay," "horse blanket," and "barnyard." Some brewers add fruit to sour beers, which complement them well. Commercial examples: Cantillon Gueuze, The Bruery Hottenroth, Duchess De Bourgogne. No craft examples in North Carolina, though they pop up occasionally, and though many are in the works.

THE MOUNTAINS

Nantahala Brewing Company in Bryson City

Nantahala Brewing Company

61 Depot Street
Bryson City, NC 28713
828-488-BEER (2337)
E-mail: ken@nantahalabrewing.com
Website: http://www.nantahalabrewing.com
Hours (fall): Monday, Thursday, and Friday, 4 P.M.–10 P.M.;
  Saturday–Sunday, noon–10 P.M.; verify seasonally
Tours: By appointment
Owner: Ken Smith
Brewmaster: Greg Geiger
Opened: 2009

Regular beer lineup: Noon Day IPA, Bryson City Brown,
  Appalachian Trail Extra (ATX) Pale Ale

Seasonals: Depot Street Summer Wheat, Up River Amber,
  Dirty Girl Blonde, Take Out Stout, Nanny Gold, Nantahala
  Pale Ale, Wet Hop Noon Day IPA, Rivers End Oktoberfest

Nantahala Brewing Company is North Carolina's westernmost
brewery. It is tucked far into the Great Smoky Mountains
in downtown Bryson City, now a major outdoor tourism destination. Bryson City is located just a few miles from both the start of
the Blue Ridge Parkway and the oldest Cherokee Indian village on

The bar at Nantahala Brewing Company

record, dating back thousands of years. The brewery is named after the Nantahala River, a whitewater-rafting destination known for its many rapids. The river even serves as a training ground for Olympic athletes.

The brewery is housed in an old Quonset hut left by the government after the Army Corps of Engineers built nearby Fontana Dam. It stands directly across the street from the Great Smoky Mountains Railway depot, where tourists can ride the old railway into the mountains on day trips. From the front deck of the brewery, patrons can watch as the old steam engines roll into the station.

The building stands next to Mike Marsden's bar "Across the Trax." Marsden had always thought it would be a great place for a brewery. That's when he met Chris and Christina Collier, a homebrewing couple who dreamed of opening their own brewery. Soon, the three were sketching up plans. A short year later, Nantahala Brewing Company opened its doors, brewing on used equipment from South Carolina's RJ Rockers brewpub.

The brewery has an enormous tasting room that opened in 2011. Its indoor façade—complete with a two-story balcony, siding, a shingled roof, and an awning over the long bar that runs in front of the entire brewery—makes patrons feel as if they're outside,. Tall tables and multiple places for games including darts and cornhole dot the brewery. A projection television decorates one wall, complementing the two flat-screen televisions over the bar.

Nantahala opened in 2009 and added its taproom in 2010. Its beers are now distributed around the state of North Carolina.

Craft beer at its source

WHAT IS CRAFT BEER?

The Brewers Association, the professional association of brewers and breweries, defines a craft brewer as small, independent, and traditional.

Small: Based on taxation laws, a small brewery is one that makes under 6 million barrels of beer per year. Very few small breweries come anywhere near that mark. The 10 largest craft brewers in the country averaged 460,000 barrels in 2010.

Independent: A brewery must not be owned or controlled by another alcoholic industry member that is itself not a craft brewer.

Traditional: A brewery must have an all-malt flagship beer or have at least 50 percent of its volume in all-malt beers or in beers that use adjuncts to enhance, rather than lighten, flavor.

The following market segments are defined within the category of "craft beer":

Microbrewery: A brewery that makes less than 15,000 barrels of beer each year. Most small breweries in the country are microbreweries.

Regional brewery: A brewery that makes between 15,000 and 6 million barrels of beer each year.

What defines a craft beer, however, is ultimately in the mind of the beer drinker. For many people, craft is about having a full-flavored beer. For others, it's about artisan craftsmanship, or about breweries that use the best possible ingredients. As more of the large beer companies produce craft-style beers, an increasingly common discussion point centers around what exactly makes a beer a craft beer. In the end, it is up to you.

Frog Level Brewing Company

56 Commerce Street
Waynesville, NC 28786
E-mail: froglevelbrewing@gmail.com
Website: http://www.froglevelbrewing.com
Owner and brewmaster: Clark Williams
Opened: 2011

Frog Level, says brewmaster and owner Clark Williams, is a reference to the frost line on the mountains that rise around Waynesville. Above the frost line, frogs can't live, but below the line, they thrive. In the bottom of the valley along the banks of Richard Creek, where Frog Level Brewing Company makes its home, it must be very froggy indeed.

Another story says that the Frog Level section of Waynesville is so nicknamed because of historical flooding. It's a part of this small mountain town that's been going through a resurgence, and Williams is in the middle of it with his brewery.

Williams is a retired marine who has his priorities in line. "Beyond my wife and family," he says, "I have two loves—this town and this state. I'll do whatever I can to help the things I

The brewing system at Frog Level Brewing Company

love. If having a brewery here means that five guys who have never been to Waynesville before come into town to try a beer, go next door and get a cup of coffee, and head down the street for a sandwich, well, that's five guys that weren't here before helping the community."

Frog Level Brewing Company is a nanobrewery, and one of the state's smallest. Williams brews on a system built out of half-barrel kegs, making 10 gallons of beer at a time. He brews twice a day, three days a week—an enormous amount of work for such a small amount of beer, but he's happy about it. He came up with the idea while traveling with his wife on a vacation to New Mexico. "I kept coming across all of these small breweries," he says. "Just really small places—though not this small—with guys working their butts off, but they were happy. When we came home, I realized, *I've got to do this.*"

The beautiful space he occupies in Waynesville—in the Frog Level section—once served as a carriage house and stable for the Vanderbilts from nearby Asheville. It's a long, century-old building with rough, exposed bricks along one side and deep red walls and brightly polished timbers along the other. A high bar runs around the brewery toward the back of the building and empties onto a large back deck that overlooks Richard Creek. The large pieces of art that span the walls and flow up into the space came from a local gallery that had to close. Williams couldn't bear to see the community lose the business, so he offered up his wall space. The art adds to the comfortable atmosphere of the tasting room and shows the close connection between this brewery and the Frog Level community.

The long hallway leading from the street to the bar at Frog Level Brewing Company

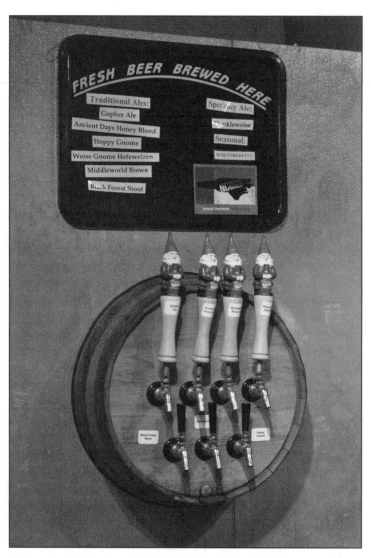

Gnomes decorate the taps at Heinzelmännchen Brewery.

Heinzelmännchen Brewery

Established 2004
Downtown Sylva, NC

Heinzelmännchen Brewery

545 Mill Street
Sylva, NC 28779
828-631-4466
E-mail: gnome@yourgnometownbrewery.com
Website: http://www.yourgnometownbrewery.com
Hours: Monday–Saturday, 10 A.M.–6 P.M.
Tours: By appointment
Owners: Dieter Kuhn and Sheryl Rudd
Brewmaster: Dieter Kuhn
Opened: 2004

Regular beer lineup: Ancient Days Honey Blonde Ale,
   Gopher Ale, Middleworld Brown Ale, Black Forest Stout,
   Weise Gnome Hefeweizen, Hoppy Gnome

Seasonals: Gnutty Gnome, Roktoberfest, Kilted Gnome
   Scottish Ale, Chocolate Covered Gnome, Imperial Gnome
   Ale, Dunkel Weise, Big Amber Gnome

Dieter Kuhn, Heinzelmännchen's *braumeister,* was born and raised in Heidelsheim, Germany, a village located near the Black Forest. As the legend goes, the Heinzelmännchen—little gnomes that garden gnomes (yes, with the red pointy hats) are modeled after—used to come out of the forest at night and do work so that the townspeople could relax all day. One night, a curious villager who wanted to see what the Heinzelmännchen looked like scattered peas on the floor of a workshop so they would slip and fall. Insulted and angry, the Heinzelmännchen never returned, leaving the people to do all the work themselves.

Kuhn sees the legend a little differently. In fact, he takes inspiration from the gnomes. "The Heinzelmännchen were helpers. They teach us that if we all help each other, life is much better. It's a sort of 'pay it forward' kind of thing."

Kuhn came to the United States via Chicago and entered the Marine Corps out of high school. It was while traveling between Chicago and his marine base on the East Coast that he discovered the mountains of western North Carolina. "It was sort of a halfway point," he says. "I used to camp here while I was traveling. It really reminded me of home, in Germany. I knew it was a place that I wanted to be with my family."

He finally moved to Sylva in 1991, but as beautiful as the mountains were, the small, isolated communities lacked one thing: good beer. "In Germany, beer was part of life," Kuhn says. "There was always beer at the table."

Remembering that his father used to make beer at home, he set out to do the same. He found a store that sold malt syrup, a health-food store that sold hops as a sleep aid, and a local bakery from which he could get yeast. The results, he says with a laugh, were horrible. "It didn't taste anything like beer!"

Knowing he could do better, he pursued higher-quality ingredients via mail order and started making much-improved beer. Friends loved it and began urging him to start his own brewery. Over time, a group of them agreed to invest in Kuhn and help him start a business. He attended the Siebel Institute in Chicago and was ready to hit the ground running.

When he returned to North Carolina, though, he found that the process was considerably more expensive than he had thought it was going to be, so he started looking at ways to cut costs. That's when he discovered Specialty Products International, a company that produces malt extract for the Beadle Brewing System, specialty brewpub equipment that requires no mashing and no lautering. Kuhn wasn't entire-

Heinzelmännchen
Brewery in Sylva

ly convinced, but after trying some of the beers and ensuring that he was receiving only the freshest extract, he moved forward, using his knowledge of brewing to supplement the extracts with specialty grains. Heinzelmännchen was off the ground.

Now, seven years later, Kuhn has a seven-barrel mash tun/lautertun in place and a plan for further growth. "I need to move out of here to expand production," he says, gesturing to the small storefront his brewery currently occupies. "I'm full."

The brewery is compact, yet comfortable. As guests walk in through the beveled-glass doors, the bulk of the brewery is laid out in front of them. A combination cash register/work desk is to the right, and a rack of local goods and, yes, garden gnomes is on the left. Just past the mash tun is a wide table in front of the cold room. The front of the cold room has taps sticking out of it through the end of a barrel. And in the middle of it all stands Kuhn, warmly welcoming guests into his brewery and offering samples.

Brewmaster Dieter Kuhn welcomes guests at Heinzelmännchen Brewery.

Literature posted around the brewery proclaims Heinzelmännchen as "Beer for food." Kuhn's beers are mostly traditional German beers or variations on other styles made to more closely resemble those traditional German beers. He talks about how he's made an IPA using malts from a maltster near his hometown in Germany, and how he uses pilsner malt and German and English hops to get more of the crisp dryness he prefers in his beer, a theme that is constant throughout each of his offerings, whether it be his seasonal Dunkel Weisse or his Black Forest Stout.

In the center of the brewery is a table covered with binders showing pictures of Sylva and of Heinzelmännchen at local events. Kuhn's goal of bringing good beer to the North Carolina mountains has also led to fruitful relationships among the brewery, the community, and the tourists who travel here for the beer.

The Heinzelmännchen would no doubt approve.

Wedge Brewing Company

125 B Roberts Street
Asheville, NC 28801
828-505-2792
E-mail: info@wedgebrewing.com
Website: http://wedgebrewing.com
Hours: Monday–Thursday, 4 P.M.–10 P.M.;
  Friday, 3 P.M.–10 P.M.;
  Saturday–Sunday, 2 P.M.–10 P.M.
Owner: Tim Schaller
Brewmaster: Carl Melissas
Opened: 2008

Regular beer lineup: Witbier, Julian Prince Pilsner, Payne's Pale Ale, "Derailed"-Hemp Ale, Doppelbock, Belgian Abbey Ale, Iron Rail IPA

Wedge Brewing Company is situated in the River Arts District, which is artsy and funky even by Asheville standards. It is an area known for its wide range of artists' studios. A simple sign painted on a beam leaning over the sidewalk reads, "Wedge In Back." There, a staircase leads down into a sculptor's wonderland of art and to Wedge Brewing Company.

Sculptures outside Wedge Brewing Company in Asheville

The brewing company is named after the building it's in—Wedge Studios. Much of the building stands in tribute to its late owner, John Payne, a metal artist, sculptor, engineer, and inventor.

Wedge Brewing Company's owner, Tim Schaller, moved from Sag Harbor, New York, where he had worked as a contractor renovating historic houses. In Asheville, he saw opportunity. "I built some new houses down here," he says, "but I got out at the right time."

He arrived in Asheville just after Highland Brewing Company opened its doors and has always been a fan of beer. "What got me into beer was beer," he says with a smile. "I like it. I've always been an entrepreneur of some sort, so I just took the idea of a brewery and ran with it. I usually sort of run with an idea until something comes up to stop me, but we didn't really run into any roadblocks."

He was good friends with Payne and talked to him about the possibility of the basement space. He speaks fondly of the River Arts District. "To me, this area is like the last frontier of Asheville—the last area where it's fairly local," he says. "And artists are interesting people to be around.

I liked the idea of an old man's democratic bar, where you sit around and just have conversations. And that was the idea."

Schaller found a local brewer—Carl Melissas, previously of Green Man Brewery—who was interested. He also located a good deal on equipment from a brewery in Florida. Payne, unfortunately, died a few weeks after the brewery opened.

The original idea for the basement space was that it would function primarily as a warehouse. But since the opening in 2008, it has turned into a community gathering space. Wedge Brewing Company is still trying to keep up with demand. For a time, Schaller says, Wedge built up 40 to 45 restaurants it distributed beer to, but it has since pulled back. It's now down to six or eight. The company sells all the rest of its beer on-site.

Schaller now sees Wedge Brewing Company as subsidizing the artists who continue to work in his late friend's studios. "Wedge is able to pay twice the rent that the artists can, so it's still a good deal for them," he says. "We're in a transition time, and we're trying to steer it so that maybe we can get a restaurant down here or something, and that'll pay more rent again, so that maybe the artists can stay."

A view of fermentation vessels behind the bar at Wedge

The brewhouse at Wedge

Aside from making Wedge even more community friendly, Schaller has no serious plans for growth. "I'm 65," he says, "and I can make a living. We have a small system with no real room to grow in the space, so we're not looking at getting any bigger than this. People like our beer and like our scene, and that's the main thing to us."

Wedge Brewing Company lives up to its building's legacy. The beautiful space, used for produce storage in the 1930s, is now surrounded by pieces of metal sculpture, many built by Payne. The bar is small but warm and accommodating, and the expansive patio overlooks the railroad, where freight trains roll by bearing load after load of wood chips. ("There goes the Great Smoky Mountains National Forest," Schaller quips.) While mostly closed off from public view, the brewery still pokes its tall, skinny fermenters over the tops of walls inside the taproom. They look very much at home among the sculptures created by the brewery owner's dear friend.

ASHEVILLE : BEER CITY USA

Every spring since 2009, Charlie Papazian—the author of *The Complete Joy of Homebrewing*, the founder and president of the Brewers Association and the American Homebrewers Association, and the godfather of the craft beer movement—has held an informal poll online to determine which city in America should be deemed "Beer City USA." The cities put up for the vote are determined by nominations from readers of Papazian's online column. They usually include Philadelphia, San Diego, St. Louis, San Francisco, Oakland, Seattle, Denver, Milwaukee, Portland, Oregon, and Fort Collins, Colorado, among many others.

Once the cities are determined, voting commences for a week, at the end of which the city with the highest number of votes is declared Beer City USA. In 2009, Asheville finished in a tie with Portland. In 2010, Asheville won again, with Portland as its closest competitor. In 2011, Asheville reigned supreme, crushing its closest competitor, San Diego, by amassing over twice as many votes.

Being proclaimed Beer City USA says more about Asheville than just the quality of its beer. It is more than rating hop choices, alcohol percentage, recipes, and flavor profiles. It suggests a supportive community with local pride for Asheville and for North Carolina beer.

See more about Beer City USA online at examiner.com/tag/beercity-usa.

Craggie Brewing Company

197 Hilliard Avenue
Asheville, NC 28801
828-254-0360
E-mail: contact@craggiebrewingco.com
Website: http://www.craggiebrewingco.com
Hours: Tuesday–Thursday, 4 p.m.–9 p.m.;
  Friday–Saturday, 4 p.m.–10 p.m.
Tours: By appointment
Owners: Bill Drew and Jonathan Cort
Brewmaster: Bill Drew
Opened: 2007

Regular beer lineup: Burning Barrel, Dubbelicious,
  Antebellum Ale, Toubab Brewe

Seasonals: Germinator Doppelbock, Herkulean IPA, Meet
  Your Maker Barley Wine, White Squirrel, Swannanoa
  Sunset, Battery Hill

When asked how he got into beer, Bill Drew has a simple one-word answer: "Boredom."

As an Elon University psychology student, Drew learned quite

Art decorates the wall outside Craggie Brewing Company.

a bit about beer in his travels overseas. He spent time in Scotland, London, Amsterdam, France, and elsewhere in Europe. When he returned to the United States, he found that just as much beer was available to him right at home. He remembers the first beer he fell in love with: Dixie Voodoo Blackened Lager. He got the idea that he wanted to make something like that.

Like a good student should, Drew used the computers in the library at Elon to research everything he could about beer, grains, malt, yeast, and hops. A friend of his father knew the owner of a brewery that was opening in Asheville—a little place called Highland Brewing Company, which was to operate in the basement of a bar downtown. One of the owners said that if Drew wanted to, he could come, take a look, and volunteer to see if brewing was something he really wanted to get into. He did, and it stuck. His curiosity about beer turned into a passion, and he spent the next four years working at Highland.

Soon after that, Drew enrolled in the short course at the Siebel Institute—to learn "to dot the i's and cross the t's," he says. He then re-enrolled at Elon to get a business degree. Soon afterward, he got a job at Dogwood Brewing Company in Atlanta, Georgia. But Asheville kept calling him home. In 2005, he returned to Highland and helped the

The taproom at Craggie Brewing Company

company complete a move from its basement location to the large manufacturing facility it now inhabits.

In 2007, Drew went to Oktoberfest in Munich. "It's time," he finally decided while he was there. When he returned from his trip, he started Craggie Brewing Company.

Like many small breweries, Craggie is essentially a one-man operation. Drew does the lion's share of the work and has help only on tasks that would take forever if he had to do them alone. What makes Craggie stand apart is Drew's view of beer.

"I had to find a niche," he says. "There are so many breweries up here, and I didn't want to do what everybody else is doing. Nobody needs another Asheville lager, or Asheville amber, or porter, or stout. So I take recipes and try to switch it up a little bit—instead of making just a normal lager, making a zwickelbier or a kellerbier or that sort of thing. And our amber is our Antebellum Ale, which is not a normal amber. I'm more of a creative brewer. To me, when you break down the science and get too specific, it almost takes the fun out of it."

Antebellum Ale, though, is actually from his business partner, Jonathan Cort. It's a traditional North Carolina beer recipe. The family Cort married into had North Carolina roots stretching back to ancestors who fought in the French and Indian War. As a reward from the British, the family was granted land in North Carolina. During the Great Depression, they tried to build a brewery using a former grain mill, but they never got it off the ground.

Cort approached his aunt to see if any old recipes were left over from the brewer. She couldn't find anything from the brewery but did locate some old homestead recipes. Drew felt that one in particular was translatable to a modern palate. It was a simple recipe of just molasses, spruce, ginger, water, and yeast—no malt, no hops. Chances are that it wouldn't have resembled anything people now think of as beer. So he tweaked the recipe for a modern audience, giving it a base of malt and adding just enough hops to make it resemble a 21st-century ale. And so Antebellum Ale, Craggie's flagship, was born. It now uses significantly less molasses than the original recipe did, and just a small amount of ginger root. The spruce tips actually come from the trees in Drew's yard.

"We like full, well-balanced flavor that's not really in your face," he says. "When you drink Antebellum Ale, some people pick out the molasses, some people pick out the ginger, others pick out the spruce." It

Fermenters at Craggie Brewing Company

is a perfect representation of one of Craggie's early mottos: "Tradition Transformed."

Drew and Cort are happy with Craggie's success and would like to see it grow. But after Drew's experience with bottling at Highland, they're not entirely sure they want to make the jump to packaging. "It was a great experience for me as a prospective brewery owner to witness Highland's growing pains," says Drew.

For now, they're working to expand their distribution to other parts of North Carolina and are looking at expanding into Tennessee as well.

Asheville Pizza and Brewing Company

Coxe Avenue location:

77 Coxe Avenue
Asheville, NC 28801
828-255-4077
Hours: Monday–Thursday, 11 a.m.–midnight; Friday, 11 a.m.–2 a.m.;
    Saturday, noon–2 a.m.; Sunday, noon–midnight

Merrimon Avenue location:

675 Merrimon Avenue
Asheville, NC 28804
828-254-1281
Hours: Daily, 11 a.m.–midnight

Website: http://ashevillebrewing.com
Tours: Through Brews Cruise, Inc. (brewscruise.com/inc/)
Head Brewer: Doug Riley
Opened: 1999

Regular beer lineup: Shiva IPA, Houdini Pale Ale, Ninja Porter, Old
    School Pale Ale, Roland ESB, Rocket Girl, Scottish, Scout Stout, Red
    Light Pale Ale

Seasonal: Christmas Jam White Ale

The kettle and mash tun at Asheville Pizza and Brewing Company

Doug Riley came to Asheville in 1998. He made the move from Portland, Oregon, where he had been a brewer for Norwester Brewing Company. He moved east to help start a brewery, but it wasn't his own. It was the third brewery to open its doors in Asheville—Two Moons Brew and View, located on Merrimon Avenue not far from UNC-Asheville.

A year later, the original owners sold it to Riley and his partners, Mike Rangel and Leigh Lewis. They merged the operation with Asheville Pizza Company, creating the successful brewpub—and now brewery chain—that has been a staple in town for over a decade.

"It's your typical brewpub movie theater," jokes Riley about Asheville Pizza and Brewing's original location. "We show second-run films and serve pizza and beer." The movie theater is what patrons would expect from a small venue—the wide white screen, the ruffled-curtain walls—but instead of rows of low-slung, upholstered movie seats, tables and chairs face the screen. It is the perfect place for a pizza and a beer while watching a movie.

The operation was so effective that the partners opened a second location closer to downtown, on Coxe Avenue, in 2006. That Asheville Pizza and Brewing is a bright pizza parlor with a light wooden motif, a long, L-shaped bar, and a large outdoor patio. It is similar to the first location but without the movies.

The second location means that Asheville Pizza doubled its brewing capacity, rather than giving itself twice as many locations to dispense the same amount of beer. "We were in pretty high demand for our beer," Riley explains, "so we expanded out of necessity. There's a second full brewery on Coxe Avenue, with about as much room in the back of the brewery as there is in the front."

Asheville Pizza has been selling its beer in 22-ounce bottles statewide for some time now. Recently, it put a canning line in place to help expand capacity. "We thought that a canning line would be a lot better—more environmentally friendly. Our beer can get into state parks, at the beach. With Asheville being such an outdoorsy town, it just made sense," Riley says.

A view of fermentation vessels past the brewhouse at Asheville Pizza and Brewing Company

After witnessing the Asheville brewing scene grow up around his brewery, Riley has one word: "Crazy. It's a small town, and it supports a lot of breweries, but we all make different types of beer, and I think there's enough for everybody to go around."

As for the future, Riley says Asheville Pizza will play it by ear. "We'll get through the winter and see how things go with cans," he says, "and see if we need to get larger from there."

RIVERBEND
MALT HOUSE

Partners Brent Manning and Brian Simpson were environmental consultants when they met. They had a common question in mind: Why was none of the barley grown in North Carolina fit for brewing beer? The answer turned out to be simple: Because people grew barley for feed, not for beer.

The partners took themselves to a professional malting school and started working with a few local farmers. They now operate North Carolina's first maltster—a "micro-maltster," they call it—Riverbend Malt House in Asheville.

Still in their early days, they are working on testing both their malting process and their end products. But they have already drawn interest from dozens of brewers throughout the Southeast and are the supplier for two 100 percent North Carolina–grown beers brewed by Weeping Radish and Mother Earth breweries.

Green Man Brewery

23 Buxton Avenue
Asheville, NC 28801
828-252-5502
E-mail: beerisgood@greenmanbrewery.com
Website: http://www.greenmanbrewery.com
Hours: Daily, 4 P.M.–9 P.M.
Tours: Part of Brews Cruise walking tour (brewscruise.com/inc/)
Owner: Dennis Thies
Brewmaster: John Stuart
Opened: 1997

Regular beer lineup: ESB, Pale, IPA, Porter

Seasonals: Rainmaker Double IPA, Easy Rider Summer Wheat, Oktoberfest, Stout, The Dweller

Green Man is Asheville's second-oldest brewery, having opened just a couple years after Highland. The brewery has been through an enormous amount of change and today is beginning to see the same growth that much of the rest of Asheville's brewing community enjoys.

For years, Green Man was part of Jack of the Wood, a downtown

Green Man Brewery in Asheville   Photo courtesy of Mia Baylor Strauss

tavern and launch point for some of Asheville's most successful brewer-
ies. Brewers from Jack of the Wood have gone on to work at—or start—
French Broad Brewing Co., Lexington Avenue Brewery, and Wedge
Brewing Company.

In 2010, Green Man was bought by Dennis Thies, a beer industry
veteran. Under Thies, Green Man found new independence from Jack
of the Wood and has started expanding operations, though it still brews
beer for the pub. In the time it took to re-license the brewery, Thies and
the team at Green Man remodeled. They also worked through the entire
beer lineup with Green Man's original brewer, John Stuart, with an eye
on quality and consistency, taking beers that were already great and fine-
tuning them for excellence.

By the end of 2010, Thies had doubled Green Man's capacity and
opened its tasting room, Dirty Jack's, which provides a relaxed atmosphere for enjoying Green Man beer and whatever soccer game is on
television. He also started Next Generation Beer Company, an accompa-
nying distributor that is in charge of getting Green Man beers—as well

as a host of others from around the country—out on the market.

Future plans for Green Man include statewide distribution and packaging in both six-packs and 750-milliliter bottles.

Green Man Brewery growlers PHOTO COURTESY OF KATHERINE BECKER

OysterHouse
Brewing Company

35 Patton Avenue
Asheville, NC 28801
828-350-0505
E-mail: billy@oysterhousebeers.com
Website: http://www.oysterhousebeers.com
Hours: Daily, 5 P.M.–11 P.M.
Owner: Amy Beard
Brewmaster: Billy Klingel
Opened: 2009

Regular beer lineup: Dirty Blonde, Patton Ave. Pale Ale,
  Upside Down Brown, Moonstone Stout, India Pale Ale

OysterHouse Brewing Company might be one of the most nontraditional breweries in North Carolina—or anywhere else, for that matter. It's not really a brewpub so much as it is a seafood restaurant that happens to make its own beer.

Billy Klingel, the brewer at OysterHouse, has worked at The Lobster Trap since before it was open. He also happens to be "a geeked-out homebrewer," in his own words. Tres Hundertmark, the original general manager and executive chef at The Lobster Trap, used to go to oyster-shucking tournaments, in which people compete to shuck the most oysters in a certain amount of time. Hundertmark

The brewing system behind the bar at The Lobster Trap,
a.k.a. OysterHouse Brewing Company

is a champion oyster shucker. After returning from a competition in
Boston back in 2006, he told Billy about a beer he had heard of while he
was there: an oyster stout.

"I had lost my overall obsession with homebrewing by that point.
It wasn't because I stopped loving doing it, I just didn't have the time,"
Klingel says. "But there we were, with a cooler with a dozen different
varieties of oysters in it on any given day, and I thought, *Well, this is my
chance*. Every homebrewer dreams about making the jump to having
their own brewery. I had always had this vision that I would have this
little pizza place, and we would make our own beer, and I might not be a
millionaire, but I'd get by, and it would be great. I thought, *Well, it's not
really the way my dream was written out, but it's certainly a great way to
start*. So I got a little obsessed again."

Over the course of the next year, he brewed 60 or so batches of
homebrew, and at least 50 of them were oyster stouts. He tweaked the
recipe each time until he thought it was just right. He brought the final

The brewing system frames the entrance to the kitchen at The Lobster Trap.

product in to his boss, Amy Beard, founder of The Lobster Trap. "At that point," says Klingel, "Amy was a Bud Select drinker. So for her to take a drink of something you can't see through and say, 'That's good!' was pretty great."

Klingel told Beard his plan and came up with a sample budget, and The Lobster Trap soon began to make its own beer. He originally tried to find a three-barrel system in hopes that he could devise some way of fitting a small brewhouse and fermenters into the restaurant, but he ended up getting a half-barrel "Brew Magic" system built from half-barrel kegs—essentially an elaborate homebrewing system. He makes about 12 gallons of beer at a time.

Wednesday, Thursday, and Friday are brew days. Klingel starts brewing at about 7 A.M. and tries to be done by 2 P.M., before the restaurant really gets going. Almost all of the beers Klingel makes in the restaurant are oyster stouts. He has contracted out other styles at French Broad Brewing Co. in Asheville. He goes to its facility about once a month and brews for the day, filling all of his own kegs with beers for the restaurant. And while they're popular and good, nothing really stands up to the oyster stout that The Lobster Trap has become famous for.

Each batch of his oyster stout contains about five pounds of un-

BREWGRASS

- When it happens: September
- Where it happens: Martin Luther King Jr. Park in Asheville
- Ticket price: About $40
- Features: 40 breweries from around the state and country, as well as regionally and nationally known bluegrass musicians
- Notes: This is a seven-hour-long music festival. Tickets sell out almost immediately each year.

shucked oysters. "The shell is the best part," Klingel says. While he has experimented with using different varieties of oysters, he's not sure that they make a significant difference. The main factor, he says, is the size. Some oysters are big and some small, so while the flavor might not change much, the cost of the beer might change dramatically.

Many people are skeptical of oyster stout, says Klingel. "They have a hard time trying it. But I tell them, 'It doesn't taste like oysters. The only reason you know there are oysters in there is because I'm telling you in case you have an allergy to shellfish.' " Nonetheless, the brewery business inside The Lobster Trap has ultimately been a success. "One day, I looked out here, and this was probably a few months after we started making beer, and the whole bar was full, all the seats were taken, and everybody at the bar except for two people had a pint of stout. This was old, young, men, women. And I thought, *I have just won.*"

Klingel says that, in the future, he'd love to see the brewery expand beyond the cramped kitchen space of The Lobster Trap. "My five-year plan—maybe—is to take this brand and these beers someplace bigger. The day that I'll be making 12 barrels of beer instead of 12 gallons, I'll be really happy."

Lexington Avenue Brewery

39 North Lexington Avenue
Asheville, NC 28801
828-252-2827
E-mail: bookings@lexavebrew.com
Website: http://www.lexavebrew.com
Hours: Monday–Saturday, 11:30 A.M.–2 A.M.; Sunday, noon–2 A.M.
Tours: Part of Brews Cruise tour (brewscruise.com/inc/)
Owners: Steve Wilmans and Mike Healy
Brewmaster: Ben Pierson
Opened: 2009

Regular beer lineup: American Pale Ale, Chocolate Stout,
    Marzenbier, Bohemian Pilsner, LAB IPA, Belgian White Ale

Award: 2011 GABF Bronze Medal for "Porter"

Steve Wilmans and Mike Healy are not typical bar owners.
Wilmans, a recording-industry veteran, was a partner
in Seattle's Stepping Stone Studios when such acts as Pearl Jam,
Soundgarden, and Modest Mouse were on their way up—that is,
he was until a Microsoft executive made him an offer he couldn't
refuse. After a year of travel, Wilmans found himself in Los Ange-

LAB, or Lexington Avenue Brewery, in Asheville

les agreeing to help Healy, a longtime friend, pick up and move across the country to Asheville. There, Wilmans fell in love with the local vibe and ended up opening a new recording studio, Echo Mountain Studios.

At the same time, Wilmans and Healy pooled their resources and bought a space in downtown Asheville. It had always been Healy's dream to open a pub, and it seemed fitting that his pub in Asheville would feature a brewery. After three full years of renovations, that space became LAB—Lexington Avenue Brewery.

To brew the beer, they hired Ben Pierson, a veteran of the Asheville brewing scene. Ben had brewed at Jack of the Wood (now Green Man) before leaving to become a brewery consultant who helped open breweries around the Southeast. This project, in a town where he had seen so much success, pulled him back.

Lexington Avenue was conceived as more than just a regular brewpub. It is a "gastropub"—a pub that pairs high-quality food with its beers. It also places an emphasis on live music. LAB features two stages—an acoustic stage in the dining area and one in the back of the brewpub that's soundproof, so it can host live shows without disturbing dining patrons.

The brewhouse can be seen between lit fermenters at Lexington Avenue Brewery.

The sweeping, curved bar and the dining area are lavishly beautiful. The outdoor patio seating blends seamlessly into the brewpub's main dining area. And all of it is lit by the spectacular light show in the brewery, where colored lights are cast against the stainless-steel fermenters. Through the fermenters, the beautiful 15-barrel copper kettle brewhouse is barely visible, allowing patrons to see shadows of movement while brewing is happening in the back.

The bar at Lexington Avenue Brewery

French Broad Brewing Co.

101 Fairview Road #D
Asheville, NC 28803
828-277-0222
E-mail: andy@frenchbroadbrewery.com
Website: http://frenchbroadbrewery.com
Hours: Monday–Saturday, 1 P.M.–8 P.M.
Tours: Part of Brews Cruise tour (brewscruise.com/inc/) or by
    appointment
Owner: Andrew Dahm
Brewmaster: Chris Richards
Opened: 2001

Regular beer lineup: 13 Rebels ESB, Wee Heavy-er Scotch
    Ale, Gateway Kölsch, Rye Hopper, Anvil Porter

Seasonal: Zepptemberfest

Andy Dahm has always loved beer. After a career in printing
and graphic arts in and around the Southeast, he settled in
Asheville and started Asheville Brewing Supply in 1994. Seven
years later, when friend and local brewer Jonas Rembert decided
to move on from his post at Jack of the Wood and start his own
brewery, Dahm jumped on board, though to this day he's not sure

Fermenters at French Broad Brewing Co.

why. "I have no recollection," he says of the decision to start a brewery, "but it's a safe bet that alcohol was involved."

The brewery—one of Asheville's first, opening just a few years behind Highland—set out to make distinctive European-style lagers. It did that well and soon began expanding its repertoire. The brewery first operated as a production-only facility. In 2004, it opened a small 25-seat tasting room that has made it a popular destination, especially because of the constant schedule of live music. The intimate setting attracts some of Asheville's most popular musicians. French Broad now boasts music five nights a week.

Dahm speaks of founding brewer Jonas Rembert: "The music offerings reflect the interests of a lot of people in our company, but I'd have to say that Jonas really made the listening room part of our business happen, and we're grateful to him for getting that done."

Being one of the older breweries in town has given French Broad the ability to watch the Asheville brewing scene grow up around it, an experience Dahm calls "gratifying." Still, French Broad remains one of the

The bar at French Broad Brewing Co.

smaller breweries in town, despite the fact that it distributes throughout the state. "We're probably working with less share capitalization than most breweries in town, and we've become a very resourceful, quality-obsessed organization because of it," says Dahm.

The current head brewer, Chris Richards, was—like every brewer who has ever worked at French Broad—a homebrewer. He joined the company in 2007, shortly after Rembert's departure. Richards began working as a keg washer and cellarman under the tutelage of then–head brewer Drew Barton. Now, he works with Dahm to help the company toward its goal of new growth. French Broad has been increasing its bottling capacity to meet demand and has plans to expand the size of its taproom.

French Broad will take the future as it comes, says Dahm. "We figure that moving forward is going to happen whether we plan for it or not."

Highland Brewing Company

12 Old Charlotte Highway, Suite H
Asheville, NC 28803
828-299-7223
E-mail: info@highlandbrewing.com
Website: http://www.highlandbrewing.com
Hours: Thursday–Saturday, 4 P.M.–8 P.M.
Tours: Monday–Saturday, 4 P.M.
Owners: Oscar Wong and John Lyda
Brewmaster: John Lyda
Opened: 1994

Regular beer lineup: Gaelic Ale, Oatmeal Porter, St. Terese's Pale
Ale, Kashmir IPA, Black Mocha Stout

Seasonals: Seven Sisters Abbey-Style Dubbel, Tasgall Ale, Cold
Mountain Winter Ale, Clawhammer Oktoberfest, Cattail Peak
Wheat

Awards: 2006 World Beer Cup Silver Medal for "Black Mocha Stout"
2008 GABF Silver Medal for "Black Mocha Stout"

Highland Brewing Company is one of the oldest operating packaging breweries in North Carolina. The idea was originally that of John McDermott, who discovered beer as

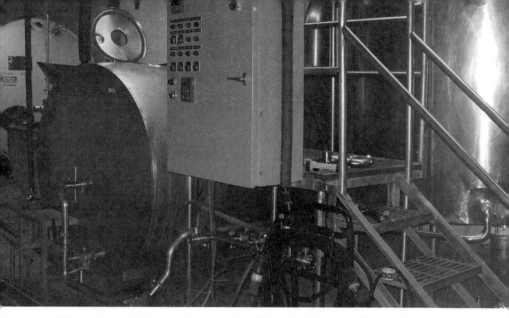

The brewhouse and fermentation operation at the original location of Highland Brewing Company Photo courtesy of Highland Brewing Company

a homebrewer in the 1980s and was in California when some of that state's first breweries and brewpubs opened. Like a few homebrewers before him and many after him, McDermott started down the road to opening his own brewing business.

First came a stint at Catamount Brewing Company in White River Junction, Vermont, where he conceived the idea of opening a brewpub in Boston. When that plan didn't come together, he moved to Baton Rouge, Louisiana, to work for the Mill Bakery, Eatery, and Brewery, a chain of health-conscious brewpubs that is (unsurprisingly) no longer in existence. He eventually transferred to a branch of the brewery in Charlotte and also worked part-time at nearby Dilworth Brewing Company.

While in Charlotte, McDermott came across an ad in an agricultural magazine for some used dairy equipment. He decided to go for it, figuring he could use his experience and his background in mechanical engineering to retool the equipment into whatever he might need for a brewery.

Meanwhile, Oscar Wong was looking for a good business investment. Wong was living in Charlotte after a successful career as a completely different type of entrepreneur, having built his own engineering firm. When his company was bought out and the Charlotte branch closed, Wong was "coasting, cooking, and volunteering." A friend introduced him to McDermott, who needed backing to start his brewery. "I always appreciated beer," says Wong, "and I needed a hobby. My wife was glad to see me out of the house."

At the time, they felt the Charlotte market couldn't support another brewery, so they decided on Asheville as a startup location. They found a space beneath Universal Pizza and Barley's Taproom and set up shop, albeit slowly. The cramped location needed a fair amount of refurbishment, and city inspectors who had never dealt with a brewery before gave them a bit of a hard time, but they eventually became Asheville's first legal brewery since Prohibition.

John Lyda, now Highland's director of brewing, was their first employee. He looks back at the early days with a shake of his head. "It was a big challenge, especially with sanitation. We were in the basement of a bar, so there was dust being kicked up all over the place."

Wong adds a little spice to the story. "Cleaning out the tanks by hand meant a brewer going shirtless. Somehow, visitors who saw the naked top half of a brewer would, for some reason, assume that he was fully naked. We weren't too quick to deny that."

In addition, they were using equipment that was not made for brewing beer. Their mash tun was a 35-barrel Sealtest ice-cream pasteurizer with steam pipes running through the middle of it for heat. Their fermenters were 2,000-gallon dairy tanks.

Wong has many stories of the initial challenges. He's particularly proud of Highland's Oatmeal Porter because "it was born under duress." After three 2,000-gallon batches of lager ended up in the sewer and a fourth was not quite up to par, they designed a dark beer to incorporate some of the lager. "We still had to dump most of it, because we didn't have sufficient sales," says Wong, "but it is now Highland's second-highest-selling beer," behind its Gaelic Ale. Oatmeal Porter no longer contains any lager.

A couple of years after opening, Highland started packaging 22-ounce bottles. "We didn't have equipment that gave us confidence in the filling process," Wong remembers, "so we pasteurized them in an open milk tank." They would place about 1,300 bottles in layers in the tank and pump water through it, starting cold, slowly raising the

The bar in the taproom at Highland Brewing Company

temperature to about 160 degrees Fahrenheit, and then slowly reducing the temperature again. "We would lose up to 40 bottles each time, and a good day was 12 or less."

Lyda joined the brewery in the way many did in the 1990s. He was a homebrewer who wanted to do more. His mother had bought him a homebrewing kit at a church rummage sale when he was in college because she saw him spending so much money on Belgian beers, his favorites. He fell in love with homebrewing and, with a buddy who was a restaurateur, laid plans to open a cinema draft house. But Lyda wanted to go to brewing school and do things right. The Siebel Institute required three years of professional experience at that point, "so I figured I'd just keep beating on Highland's door," he recalls. After 10 years of homebrewing, his first brewery job proved to be his only brewery job.

While Lyda was away taking his brewery course, trouble was brewing back at Highland, which was having problems with consistency in its beer. Lyda talks about what happened with Highland's original brewer: "McDermott was always more of an artist. He was a great brewer, but he had a habit of changing recipes, and not in a subtle way, and it wasn't very good for consistency. It was no fault of his. He just wasn't happy as an artist." When Lyda returned from his brewing course, Wong approached him with an idea. Together, they bought McDermott out of the brewery. "The focus from the beginning for us was quality and consistency," says Lyda.

Highland continued to grow at a breakneck pace. It quickly reached its full capacity at its basement facility—about 6,500 barrels per year— and still had a hard time satisfying demand. It became obvious that the brewery needed a larger plant. But Lyda and Wong didn't want to move and immediately have the same capacity problems, so they shot big.

They began to contract their bottle accounts out of Frederick Brewing Company in Maryland while still satisfying keg accounts from their production facility in the basement of Barley's. They used the contracted bottles to grow their distribution to a point they could easily match with a larger system. Meanwhile, they built their new brewery in a building that once housed Blue Ridge Motion Pictures.

Their brewery now resembles a large manufacturing facility, in sharp contrast to the old cobbled-together basement operation. The

The brewhouse at Highland Brewing Company

50-barrel brewhouse has row upon row of 100-barrel tanks that tower throughout the giant warehouse. The constant rattle of the bottling line serves as a soundtrack as Highland's crew fills case after case of beer, ready for distribution.

Highland's tasting room is bigger than many of the state's smaller breweries. It has a long bar, hundreds of seats, and a stage for presentations and performances, all hemmed in by converted railroad cars that act as offices for some of the brewery's staff. What's more, the brewery still has plenty of room to grow in the tens of thousands of square feet it hasn't put to use yet.

Although the brewery's future is bright, Lyda says Highland is not necessarily after a national brand. "We want to stay regional," he says. But since craft beer is still only a small percentage of the market, regional operations like Highland have the opportunity for an enormous amount of growth.

Hendersonville, North Carolina

Southern Appalachian Brewery

822 Locust Street
Hendersonville, NC 28792
E-mail: mail@sabrewery.com
Website: http://www.sabrewery.com
Hours: Wednesday–Friday, opens at 4 P.M.; Saturday–Sunday, opens at 2 P.M.
Owners: Andy and Kelly Cubbin
Brewmaster: Andy Cubbin
Opened: 2003

Regular beer lineup: Belgian Blonde Ale, Copperhead Amber Ale, India Pale Ale, Black Bear Stout

When Andy and Kelly Cubbin first considered getting into brewing, they didn't even live in North Carolina. The couple was in Chicago, working as photographers and looking for a change. Andy had been homebrewing for years. When they found a brewery for sale in Rosman, North Carolina, they decided to jump at the chance to get out of the city.

The property they bought was Appalachian Brewery. "It was really small," says Andy, "somewhere between a nano and a micro. It was a five- or six-barrel Frankensteined kind of system, basically

A view of fermentation at Southern Appalachian Brewery

like a small homebrewing operation." But it gave him something to cut his teeth on. The couple renamed the place Appalachian Craft Brewery, to try to distinguish it from Appalachian Brewing Company in Harrisburg, Pennsylvania. The couple moved the brewery to Fletcher and started making beer.

It was not at that point a full-time undertaking. Unsure that the small brewery was going to support them, they kept pursuing photography. But over the next four years of brewing and perfecting recipes, they resolved to make a run at it. "We decided that we just couldn't do it halfway," says Andy. "We said to ourselves, *We're good at it. We can do it. Let's go for it.*"

They immediately began looking for a larger system and a new space for the brewery. They had originally planned to move into Asheville, but during the four years the Cubbins were looking at the city, four new breweries opened. So they decided to make their stand elsewhere and eventually settled on Hendersonville. It was a town they liked and could see themselves living in. It was also close enough to Asheville to still be part of the "Beer City" phenomenon. And they found what they describe as "the perfect space." They bought a new, better, larger system and started the move.

Since the brewery wasn't their primary source of income, they closed it to move. "We basically said to people, 'We're going to be gone for a while. I hope you put us back on tap,' " recalls Andy. They also renamed the brewery yet again, to distance it further from Appalachian Brewing Company. "People recognized us as Appalachian Craft Brewery, so we needed it to be similar. But it was still an issue, so we renamed it Southern Appalachian Brewery, really, to get to the other end of the alphabet."

What followed were six months of bureaucratic delays. By April 2011, they were back in business, with a whole new set of challenges. "Now, we're running a bar," says Andy. "We've never done that before, so every day is a new learning experience."

Andy is a self-taught brewer, and he's proud of that fact. "I think that there are two types of brewers," he says, "some who follow the science of brewing, and some that live in the art and the craft of it. If you can make good beer, you can always learn more of the science. But I think

Patrons enjoying themselves at Southern Appalachian Brewery

Band playing at Southern Appalachian Brewery

the hardest thing about brewing, just like it is with cooking, is being able to taste something and then improve upon it."

The Cubbins look forward to having the first full year of the brewery under their belts. "It'll be great when the focus gets to become a little bit more about the beer," says Andy, who currently fills the roles of accountant, bookkeeper, delivery man, and head brewer. "We're looking forward to working with a distributor so that they can handle getting the product out and we can focus on getting it made."

HOP FARMING

Due to the growth of the craft beer industry, the state's farmers have increasingly looked toward hops as a crop, particularly as a potential replacement for tobacco. North Carolina's climate, however, poses some interesting challenges.

Van Burnette is the sole farmer at Hop 'n Blueberry Farm in Black Mountain, one of the first hop yards in North Carolina to explore the possibility of growing hops commercially. Rather than growing an extensive variety or large acreage of hops, he works closely with the North Carolina Hops Project. The project, a team effort of North Carolina State University's Departments of Soil Science and Horticultural Science, is designed to determine whether or not hops are a viable crop, what varieties can grow in the state, where the best possible geography is for hop farming, what the best strategies are for growing hops, and what problems (pests, diseases, nutrition)

Volunteers pruning hops at Hop 'n Blueberry Farm in Black Mountain
PHOTO COURTESY OF VAN BURNETTE

might arise in the state's climate. The project works with six farms around the state that grow a variety of hops. The farms serve as working labs for field researchers. For information about the North Carolina Hops Project, including some of its early results and the farms it has worked with, visit nchops.soil.ncsu.edu/nchops.

Burnette grows about a half-acre of American varieties—Cascade, Chinook, and Nugget—which seem to do better in North Carolina than European varieties. His farm is all-organic, which poses its own problems. Hops are susceptible to common garden pests and mildew. Still, those don't worry him. "It's not the heat or the humidity that hops really have a problem with down here," Burnette says. "It's the light."

Hops grow best between the 35th and 55th latitudes in both the Northern and Southern hemispheres. North Carolina just barely falls within that range. While hops have been successfully grown by hobbyists in all 50 states (which range as low as the 22nd latitude), most commercial hop farming takes place above the 45th latitude. That's because the higher latitudes get much more sunlight in the middle of summer than the lower latitudes.

Hops grow incredibly quickly. The plants die back to the ground each winter and regrow their entire length—which can be upwards of 25 feet—each summer. In addition to water and nutrients, hops require an immense amount of sunlight to achieve such growth. Burnette has noted that his hops—especially second- or third-year hops—tend to start flowering before they've achieved their full length. "The days don't get long enough for the hops to achieve their full growth before they start flowering, so we end up with smaller harvests," he says. On the other hand, long Southern summers mean multiple harvests. Most commercial facilities cut hop bines down when the flowers are ready for harvesting. Since the bines are so tall, it is difficult and time consuming to harvest the hop cones from the plants. When they're cut down, the flowers are easily threshed from the bines. Burnette harvests the first set of cones from the bines, leaves the plants up, and then reaps a smaller late-season harvest. Using those techniques, he is able to get an overall harvest close to a commercial harvest north of the 45th parallel. But he's still not quite there.

All of Burnette's hops currently go to Pisgah Brewing Company in Black Mountain for its annual fresh hop ale, appropriately named Burnette's Brew. "It's a lot of fun to bring the hops down there and throw them straight into the kettle with the guys at Pisgah, even if it does mean an entire season's worth of work is gone all at once," he says.

Burnette hopes to be able to find hops that grow better in North Carolina in the future. In the coming years, he plans to try new varieties that are reported to grow better in Southern latitudes, and he'll continue to monitor his current hops as they enter their third year of growth.

Interested parties can visit the farm and even volunteer to help out with the hop yard. Burnette notes that it takes "about one person per acre of hops" working full-time to maintain a hop yard. He welcomes help. "I'm not getting any younger," he jokes.

Among the hop farms in North Carolina are Hop 'n Blueberry Farm (hopnblueberryfarm.blogspot.com) in Black Mountain, Blue Ridge Hops (blueridgehops.com) in Marshall, Winding River Hops in Clyde, Echoview Farm (NCechoviewfarm.com) in Weaverville, and Cone & Bine Hop Farm (cbhopfarm.com) in Conover.

Pisgah Brewing Company

150 Eastside Drive
Black Mountain, NC 28711
828-669-0190
E-mail: info@pisgahbrewing.com
Website: http://pisgahbrewing.com
Hours: Monday–Wednesday, 4 P.M.–9 P.M.; Thursday–Saturday,
 2 P.M.–midnight; Sunday, 2 P.M.–9 P.M.
Tours: Saturday at 2 P.M. and 3 P.M.
Owner and brewmaster: Jason Caughman
Opened: 2005

Regular beer lineup: Pisgah Pale Ale, Summer Ale, India Pale
 Ale, Pisgah Porter, Nitro Stout, Solstice

Seasonals: Schwarzbier, Roasted Chocolate Stout, Bacon
 Stout, Apple Jaxx, Vortex I, Valdez

Beers of the past: American Pilsner, Vortex II, Baptista, Hell-
 bender Barleywine, LEAF Amber, Pisgah Equinox, Cosmos,
 Pisgah Pub Ale, San Francisco Lager, Pisgah Brown Ale, Irish
 Red Ale, Belgian Amber Ale, The Red Devil, Belgian Pale Ale,
 Abbey Ale, Reserve, German Pilsner, Saison, Pisgah Oktober-
 fest, Imperial IPA #1, Abbey, American Hefeweizen, Dancin'
 Hobo, Pisgah Château

A sunset (and a beer) at Pisgah Brewing Company Photo courtesy of Jim White

David Quinn and Jason Caughman, the founders of Pisgah Brewing Company, did not meet in business circumstances, but rather at a potluck dinner held by mutual friends in Charleston, South Carolina, where they were both living. As it happened, Quinn, a longtime brewer, had brought a keg of his pale ale to the party. The two quickly became friends. Soon, their complementary skills—Quinn's homebrew and Caughman's graphic design—led them to begin a business together. "It was a pretty typical entrepreneurial start," says Caughman. "I always wanted my own business, and to do something a little different to flee the corporate world."

The two found a small industrial space in Black Mountain. Theirs is a unique company that fits perfectly into the Asheville area's ethos. Most of Pisgah's beers are certified organic. "Occasionally, we'll do something that isn't certified but has all local honey or apples or something," says Caughman. Even when it isn't brewing organic, Pisgah still sticks to a strong commitment to buying as many of its supplies and ingredients as possible from local vendors.

Pisgah has also become known as a music venue, hosting local, regional, and national acts like Steel Pulse, Lucinda Williams, and Grace

The bar at Pisgah Brewing Company Photo courtesy of Jim White

Potter at both indoor and outdoor stages. "The music just came about," says Caughman. "I'm a music lover, so we just kind of went in that direction. We built a stage instead of buying more tanks."

The brewery is noted for its constantly rotating selection of small-batch beers. At times, a dozen or more beers are on tap in the brewery that can't be had anywhere else. "We're pretty small, but we have a tremendous amount of local support," says Caughman. "We have to continue to make new, exciting, different beers to stay engaged and stimulated. I think our customers appreciate being able to try 20 to 30 unique beers from us each year, too."

For the uninitiated, Pisgah is not easy to find. It is located in a small warehouse in an industrial park. From the outside, it could be any other office space. Once inside, though, patrons see Pisgah's true colors. Its brewhouse sits tucked inside its own separate room around the corner from the bar. The rough, black-box space with a short wooden bar is backed by more than two dozen taps. The short stage opposite the bar promises music to patrons on most nights. While seating is absent aside from stools at the bar, the taproom offers plenty of space for patrons to stand and hang out. Pisgah even has some outdoor seating for beautiful western North Carolina evenings.

Catawba Valley
Brewing Company

212 South Green Street
Morganton, NC 28655
828-430-6883
E-mail: wscottpyatt@gmail.com
Website: http://catawbavalleybrewingcompany.com
Hours: Wednesday–Friday, 5 P.M.–11 P.M.
Owner and brewmaster: Scott Pyatt
Opened: 1999

Regular beer lineup: Farmer Ted's Farmhouse Cream
  Ale, Brown Bear Ale, Firewater Indian Pale Ale, Honest
  Injun Stout, Indian Head Red Ale, White Zombie Ale

Seasonals: King Don's Pumpkin Ale, King Coconut Porter,
  Hyper Monkey Java Stout

Scott Pyatt didn't plan to open a brewing company. He used to homebrew with his brother, Billy, back in the 1990s. "It was something that we did on the weekends, just to hang out," he says. "Then people start telling you that your beer is great, and you just get this idea in your head. Honestly, he really wanted to do it more than I did. I wanted to get into manufacturing, but not into malt beverages." But he helped his brother get a brewery off

The brewhouse at Catawba Valley Brewing Company

the ground before Billy took a corporate move out of state. Scott stayed home, finished the facility, and started operation in nearby Glen Alpine.

Catawba Valley Brewing Company began as a one-man operation in the basement of an antique mall. After a year or two, Pyatt could afford to ditch his '69 GMC pickup truck and buy a van as he started driving and selling a lot more. He looks back at those beginnings with a grin. "If I would have known then what I know now, I never would have tried to do what I did with what I had," he says. "We started off with pure junk. It was just stuff we cobbled together. We were both fairly accomplished engineers, so we purpose-built stuff, and we'd take stuff that we liked and convert it into something that we could use. A lot of people probably couldn't make good beer with what we had, and I'm glad we don't have to make good beer on it anymore, because it was a whole lot of work."

Fortunately for Pyatt, the late 1990s were rough for the craft beer industry, so he was able to pick up good used equipment from breweries in other parts of the country that were closing. As he did, Catawba Valley was able to grow. Almost a decade later, that growth took him out of the basement brewery and down the road to Morganton. The brewery moved into a much larger space with its own interesting history. In the 1950s, the warehouse space had served as a showroom for Heritage-Henredon Furniture Industries' collection of Frank Lloyd Wright–designed furniture, known as "the Taliesin Ensemble." In the 1970s and 1980s, it was a "Wild West nightclub" called Slick Willy's.

In 2007, when Catawba Valley Brewing Company moved in, Pyatt managed to incorporate the best aspects of the building's long history into its new life as a brewery. The facility is not just a brewery but also a large tasting room and bar. Tables and chairs take up most of the available space in the warehouse. A long bar reaches from the brewing area in the back of the space toward a row of garage doors that stand open

Fermenters at Catawba Valley Brewing Company

on warm evenings. The brewery space is compact and efficient. Tall fermentation tanks are lined up against the back wall of the brewery, with natural light from the old wire-framed windows spilling over them.

Catawba Valley Brewing Company has become a community hangout and a place to hear good live music. Pyatt has put effort into building a full stage opposite the bar. "If I get interested in something, I like to support it, so we have a great music program," he says. "We have better equipment here than most bands do. We try to make it a pleasure to put on a show here."

The brewery offers an open mic night every week and has welcomed regional and national acts. It also plays host to a large number of community events such as birthday parties and weddings. "I guess we've done everything here except for a wake," says Pyatt. One of his favorite annual events is the brewery's Super Bowl party. Since Catawba Valley doesn't serve food, guests can bring their own. As people arrive to watch the Super Bowl on the projector screen, "it just turns into this huge potluck supper where people are sharing what they made with everybody and having a great time."

But of all the things Pyatt is interested in and supports, what is most important to him is his team. "One of the things that happens that really shows me that I'm doing something right is when you look at your employees, and you've got employees who are getting married, they're raising families, they're buying cars, they're buying houses, and you're expanding your brewery family. Having employees that can count on you and work not just for you but with you. You know you're really making it then."

For now, the future doesn't hold many big changes for Pyatt—just steady growth. For a while, he looked at getting into canning and even went so far as to purchase canning equipment, but "I just don't have the fermentation space to support it," he says. His plans include expanding distribution into the Charlotte area and further improving the brewery's performance space.

Olde Hickory Brewery

222 Union Square
Hickory, NC 28601
828-322-1965
E-mail: info@oldehickorytaproom.com
Website: http://www.oldehickorybrewery.com
Hours: Daily, 11 A.M.–2 A.M.
Tours: Upon request; large groups should schedule ahead of time
Owners: Steve Lyerly and Jason Yates
Brewmaster: Steve Lyerly
Opened: 1994

Regular beer lineup: Imperial Stout, Piedmont Pilsner, Table Rock Pale Ale, Hickory Stick Stout, Doppelbock, Brown Mountain Light, Scottish Ale, Hefe-Weizen, Nut Brown Ale, Chocolate Porter, Poor Richard's Ale, Ruby Lager, Bardstown Barley Wine, Irish Walker, L2 Light Lager

Seasonals: Olde Rabbit's Foot (collaborative brew with Foothills Brewing and The Duck-Rabbit Craft Brewery), Black Raven IPA, Christmas Ale

Award: 2010 World Beer Cup Silver Medal for "Irish Walker"

Olde Hickory Tap Room in Hickory

It's impossible to go to Hickory, North Carolina, and not run across Olde Hickory somewhere—whether it's the taproom in Union Square, the old brewpub Amos Howard's out on Route 70, or the brewery itself on Third Street. All have become iconic locations in this old textile center.

Steve Lyerly moved back to North Carolina in 1994. He had spent years in Missouri during high school and then college, but a job at North Carolina State University enticed him back, and he moved to Hickory to establish residence before applying for the position. He never had that chance.

An avid homebrewer, Lyerly was excited to learn about a brewpub opening in town. He quickly visited—before it even opened its doors—to ask about volunteering some of his time. The brewpub, Amos Howard's, already had a brewer, a local man by the name of Jim Walker who was also a homebrewer. In fact, Walker ran something of a homebrew supply shop out of his basement.

As it turned out, being a full-time brewer wasn't in the cards for Walker. He already held a full-time job, and he and his wife had just had

Barrels outside the testing room at Olde Hickory Brewery

twins. "The job was sold to him as, 'You can just come in on Saturdays and make some beer,' but it just doesn't work that way commercially," says Lyerly. "So Jim got frustrated very quickly and decided that it just wasn't what he wanted to do. I just ended up being the only person left standing in the building who knew anything about beer, and I talked the ownership into giving me a shot."

The brewery didn't exactly have the best possible equipment. In fact, the owners of Amos Howard's had bought reclaimed dairy equipment from Highland Brewing Company in Asheville—the same equipment John McDermott, Highland's first brewer, had adapted for use in its first facility. Some of it still resides at Amos Howard's today.

Soon after Amos Howard's opened, Lyerly met the person who would eventually become his business partner. Jason Yates was an engineer at a textile mill in nearby Morganton, where, Lyerly says, "they had a huge boneyard full of stainless-steel tanks perfect for a brewery." The two of them started planning a joint venture in which they would open their own operation not as a brewpub but as a packaging brewery. The

Amos Howard's brewpub in Hickory—the original site of Olde Hickory Brewery

owners of Amos Howard's, however, caught wind of the plan and made an offer instead. Almost a year after Amos Howard's opened, Lyerly and Yates bought it from the original six investors. They had their brewery.

Soon after the purchase, the pair also bought a little deli in a historic building in downtown Hickory's Union Square and started renovating it. After about a year and a half of remodeling, they opened the Olde Hickory Tap Room. Today, the taproom, a prominent location on the square, is often filled to the brim with happy patrons. It's a warm, welcoming environment with one full room of comfortable tables and booths and a long, dimly lit bar featuring a couple of dozen taps, liquor, and rows of pewter mugs hanging ready for the regulars they belong to.

Opening the taproom, Lyerly says, completely drained their capacity at Amos Howard's. That's when they started looking to expand into a production facility. They found another space and opened the packaging facility on Third Street in 2000, starting with used equipment from the Middlesex and Pilgrim brewing companies in Massachusetts.

The production brewery is like many others: lined with tanks. In fact, it has more than most breweries of its size. Olde Hickory's produc-

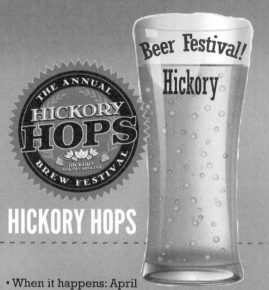

HICKORY HOPS

Paul Philippon of The Duck-Rabbit Craft Brewery shows off the Best in Show award from the Carolinas Championship of Beer at Hickory Hops.

- When it happens: April
- Where it happens: Downtown Hickory
- Ticket price: About $40
- Features: The Carolinas Championship of Beer Best in Show winners are announced during the festival; many of the winners are available for patrons to try. This festival, highly popular with the state's brewers, features one of the most complete lineups of North Carolina beers available in one place.
- Notes: This is a six-hour-long festival with limited ticket sales and bathroom facilities.

tion facility also contains its own little taproom, an array of equipment that could almost serve as a brewery museum, and barrels. Barrels are everywhere, stacked high wherever there is room for them. Not only does Olde Hickory barrel-age its own beers—its barleywine, Irish Walker, and some of its imperial stouts—it also ages Olde Rabbit's Foot, the collaborative blend it releases each year in conjunction with Foothills

Brewing and The Duck-Rabbit Craft Brewery. In addition, Lyerly has a long-term barrel-aging project in preparation for Olde Hickory's 20th anniversary in 2014. He's been aging his barleywine since 2007. By 2014, he will be able to feature a seven-year vertical of barleywines—a tasting featuring vintages from all seven years.

That's not the only project in the works. Olde Hickory has expanded production twice in the past three years and has grown its distribution around the state. In addition, Lyerly and Yates are working on their fourth location in Hickory, remodeling the old train station to create a combination bakery/deli/café that will feature 50-plus taps of craft beer, many of which, of course, will come from Olde Hickory itself.

Loe's Brewing Company

2033 North Center Street
Hickory, NC 28601
828-781-5761
E-mail: stephen@loesbrewing.com
Website: http://www.loesbrewing.com
Owners: Stephen and Robert Loe
Brewmaster: Stephen Loe
Opened: 2010

Regular beer lineup: Altered States IPA, Chocolate
  Moose XS Stout, Raspberry Wheat, Purple Thai Pale
  Ale, Fruitcake Stout, Pumpkin Ale, Vienna Zinger La-
  ger, Pull Out Red Couch Pale Ale, Southern Divinity,
  Kilt Dropper Scottish Ale, Loe's Lager, Loe's Light,
  Southern Pecan Brown

Loe's Brewing Company is one of the few truly family-operated breweries in North Carolina. Robert Loe has been homebrewing for about 40 years, says his son Stephen. "I'm 33, so I've been helping him homebrew since I was pretty little." Stephen himself started getting into homebrew around 2006. Stephen is a Culinary Institute of America graduate, and he credits that experience for pushing him toward the brewing industry. "Culinary school helped

The Loes of Loe's Brewing Company

me develop my palate," he says, "and we were starting to make some pretty good beers, so I kind of went ahead with it."

Stephen put out "maybe 75 to 100 applications" to different breweries around the country, hoping his experience as a homebrewer and his Culinary Institute degree would get him in the door somewhere. But he didn't hear back from any of them, so he decided that doing it himself—or rather, with his family—was the way to go. Today, three members of the Loe family—Robert, Stephen, and Bobby—run the brewery, all using skills they picked up through different careers to help the operation grow. All three take time on the kettle.

The brewery is tiny—just a few hundred square feet of space, with a small bar and barely enough room for the family to do the brewing. The Loes constructed most of the brewery themselves. "The idea was to partner up with the restaurant next door," says Stephen, who is still the chef

The bar in the tasting room of Loe's Brewing Company

for that restaurant, Bistro 127. "We were moving from a 1,000-square-foot restaurant to a 6,000-square-foot restaurant, and I was going to lease space for a brewery. The space was set up as a nightclub, and we had to spend three days in there with a jackhammer remodeling."

It's not a full-time job for any of the family—yet. The brewing system reflects the size of the brewery—namely, it's small. The family brews 1.5 barrels (roughly 45 gallons) at a time into five 3-barrel fermentation tanks and a couple of 1-barrel fermenters. "We tend to do large batches of the pale ale and the Vienna lager, since they're popular," Stephen says, "but we keep the rest in small batches. It keeps us flexible."

He says the family uses "overdone homebrew equipment," but it's all part of a larger plan. "We definitely want to grow," says Stephen. "We're starting to do some hand-bottling now to get into stores, and we've considered doing some contract brewing in the future until we can get our own 20-barrel system or something."

The family plans to build a restaurant with a pub-type atmosphere, which will let it put Stephen's culinary skills, Bobby's marketing skills, and Robert's brewing to work. It then hopes to get the brewing system into place once the pub is up and running.

"It was a little rough starting up," says Stephen, "but now that we got going, it's been pretty smooth sailing."

THE PIEDMONT

A view of growlers at Ass Clown Brewing Company

Ass Clown Brewing Company

17039 Kenton Drive #102
Cornelius, NC 28031
704-995-7767
E-mail: matt@assclownbeer.com
Website: http://assclownbrewery.com
Hours: Monday–Friday, 9:30 A.M.–5:30 P.M.
Owner and brewmaster: Matt Glidden
Opened: 2011

Regular beer lineup: Apricot Seed Pale Ale, Dark Chocolate
  Blueberry Porter, Peach Fig Pale Ale, Poplar Brown Ale

Seasonals: Fresh Hop Simcoe IPA, Chocolate Pumpkin
  Brown Ale, Dark Chocolate Pumpkin Porter, Pumpkin
  IPA, Coffee Tequila Oatmeal Stout, Smoked Scotch Ale,
  Hazelnut Nut Brown Ale, Smoked Maple Syrup Black
  Ale, Orange Citrus IPA, Lemon Wheat IPA, Vanilla Bean
  Chocolate Brown Ale, India Brown Ale, Dark Chocolate
  Cherry Porter

Ass Clown Brewing Company is located in just about the
last place anyone would expect: inside a mortgage company
office. When visitors approach this small brewery in Cornelius, a

Matt Glidden of Ass Clown Brewing Company

northern suburb of Charlotte, they'd never know anybody was making beer, particularly inside an office space labeled, "Interesting Mortgages."

The left side of the business is what might be expected from a mortgage company: a desk with a computer, scattered papers and pens, a rolling office chair, and a few filing cabinets. The right side, however, catches the eye in a completely different way. Small, gleaming stainless-steel fermenters are visible as soon as visitors walk in, followed by a keg box topped with a long row of taps. A wall of growlers stands next to the doorway. Everything is branded with the laughing, almost mocking visage of the Ass Clown.

"It was kind of a joke to begin with," says Matt Glidden of his company's name. Glidden is a big fan of beer festivals, but he's always had one complaint—afterward, when people asked him what he liked, he could never remember anything specific. "I thought, *If these companies would focus more on some sort of whacked-out name that I can't forget, then my chances of remembering them would be better.*" The name came to him later. "I used to have a coworker who was a good buddy that used to call me an ass clown, and I'd kind of throw it back at him, and after a while we were just calling everybody ass clowns. It was kind of catchy, and I just thought I'd see how far we could go with it."

Despite the "whacked-out" name, Glidden has serious plans for his company. His website advertises that the brewery is "small, local, and 'green,' using the best local organic ingredients (when possible)." He has plans to find local sources for hops, malt, spices, and fruits. "I'm kind of tired of drinking something or eating something with 'All Natural' just thrown up the side of it," he says. " 'All Natural,' to me, doesn't mean squat. I really like to know what's in my beer."

Drawing on his youth in Addison, Vermont, where he grew up on a farm, he already grows his own hops and uses them in some of his beers. He's also been meeting with local hops farmers and the proprietors of a new malting facility in Asheville.

Like most small brewers, Glidden started out of his garage as a homebrewer. That was back in 2003. He used to share his beer with friends and neighbors. When he noticed the crowds getting bigger and bigger, he decided to give brewing a shot, mainly as an exploratory effort.

"About three years ago, when I started looking into making the jump, I kind of knew mortgages weren't going to be around forever, so I figured it would be nice to get slowly into brewing and see if I'd fall on my ass or if I'd be able to make a decent living out of it," he says. For now, though, the mortgage company is still a primary source of income for Glidden, and one of the reasons the two businesses share offices.

As a brewer, he likes to experiment. Glidden counts Sam Calagione from Dogfish Head Brewery in Milton, Delaware, as an inspiration, even citing Calagione's startup model. "My niche is that I'm looking for an odd or a unique flavoring that's not out there." Some of the beers he has made show his love for experimentation: Apricot Seed Pale Ale, which uses both apricot fruit and pits; Dark Chocolate Blueberry Porter; Smoked Maple Syrup Black Ale; and Coffee Tequila Oatmeal Stout. Glidden says he has 40 to 50 different recipes he rotates, and that he modifies each 20 or 30 times to look for new combinations of flavors. "In my head, you don't really know what you might stumble across unless you try new things."

Fortunately, his brewery's small size allows him room to experiment.

Glidden currently brews batches of about 15 gallons at a time, using the small one-barrel fermenters in his office space. But he plans to grow. He's waiting for a 10-hectoliter system to be delivered and has found a warehouse near Charlotte that will fit his system. There, he hopes to expand not only his brewing production but also his hop growing. He says he plans to create his own "legal indoor grow room." He will also aim for environmental responsibility in his new facility, using alternative energy and recycled items including lights, furniture, and equipment.

In the future, Glidden hopes to turn the day-to-day operation of the company over to someone else while he focuses on his passion: the recipes and continued experimentation. For now, though, visitors can find him brewing in a small office inside Interesting Mortgages, a business that could not be more accurately named.

Four Friends Brewing

10913 C Office Park Drive
Charlotte, NC 28273
704-233-7071
E-mail: jon@fourfriendsbrewing.com
Website: http://www.fourfriendsbrewing.com
Tours: By appointment
Owners: Jonathan and Beth Fulcher and Mark and
   Allison Kaminsky
Brewmaster: Jonathan Fulcher
Opened: 2009

Regular beer lineup: Queen City Blonde, Queen City
   Red, Uptown Brown, Gold Rush Belgian-Style Blonde

Seasonals: Extinction Strong Ale, Dubbel D. Belgian-
   Style Dubbel

Four Friends Brewing is hidden in an office park just outside Charlotte's beltline. The entire brewery is housed in a small, one-room warehouse and is essentially a one-man operation. Jonathan Fulcher took the 2,000-square-foot space with tall ceilings and built out the brewery himself.

Fulcher was an IT guy for about 12 years. He tells of his frustration with the corporate marketplace: "Every time I'd move up the ladder, the company that I was working for would get bought out or merge with another company, and I'd have to start at the bottom again." He talked to his buddy Mark Kaminsky—they've known each other since the fifth grade—over homebrewed beers about that frustration and about how much fun it would be to run their own brewery. Kaminsky was skeptical at first, but Fulcher eventually convinced him they could make a run at it. They pooled their funds and started Four Friends, named after Fulcher and his wife, Beth, and Kaminsky and his wife, Allison.

Since they didn't really know what was needed to start a brewery, they've invented Four Friends around them as they've grown. Kamin-

A view of the taps at Four Friends Brewing

The brewhouse at Four Friends Brewing

sky, who still works at his IT job in Virginia, traveled to Charlotte to help Fulcher put the brewery together. "We built everything ourselves," Fulcher says, gesturing around the brewery. They constructed their own grain mill, their own CIP cart (a "Clean In Place" cart, including a pump and reservoirs for acid or caustic used for cleaning tanks and brewing equipment), and even their own cold room and offices. They ran their own plumbing and glycol lines and built their own bar.

It's an impressive feat in a small space. As visitors walk in, the brewhouse and fermenters stand tall above them to the right, and the bar sweeps away to the left. The cold room anchors the middle of the space. Everywhere around it is storage space stacked high to allow as much open floor as possible.

Fulcher says that running the brewery was a little rough at the beginning. "We were totally green. We knew nothing about it. We didn't know how to sell beer. We barely knew how to make it. We basically launched this on years of homebrewing. With no commercial background, everything is a learning experience, so the question really became, Can we survive long enough to learn all the lessons that need to be learned and then provide a quality product and quality service?"

He notes that, in addition, Charlotte is a tough craft market. It's a city known for NASCAR and financial institutions. Beverages tend to be split between Bud/Miller/Coors and high-end wine and spirits. "There are some beer geeks here," he says. They're incredibly supportive, "but they're scattered." Still, his beer names reflect pride in the market he's had a hard time cracking: Queen City Red, Queen City Blonde, Uptown Brown.

Now, he says, the Four Friends name is becoming known. A couple of salespeople help him get beer to the market, but Fulcher does all the deliveries himself, two days a week. It's all he can manage, since he needs to brew on the other days.

Still, for all the work, he's proud of his new profession. "This is the last bastion of manufacturing left in the country," he says. "We can't make goods in the U.S. as efficiently as we used to be able to. Craft beer is our last chance to truly be able to make and create something in this country, since it's not about making something cheap, but about making something good."

The Olde Mecklenburg Brewery

215 Southside Drive
Charlotte, NC 28217
704-525-5644
E-mail: info@oldemeckbrew.com
Website: http://oldemeckbrew.com
Hours: Tuesday–Wednesday, 4 P.M.–8 P.M.; Thursday, 4 P.M.–9 P.M.;
 Friday, 4 P.M.–10 P.M.; Saturday, noon–8 P.M.
Tours: Saturday at 2 P.M., 3 P.M., and 4 P.M.
Owner and brewmaster: John Marrino
Head brewer: Carey Savoy
Opened: 2009

Regular beer lineup: OMB Copper, OMB Mecklenburger

Seasonals: Frueh Bock, Captain James Jack Pilsner, Mecktober-
 fest, Bauern Bock, Dunkel Lager, Yule Bock

John Marrino spent 16 years in a field somewhat—but not completely—similar to beer. During his time in the water treatment
industry, he traveled all over the world, from Los Angeles to Germany to London to Charlotte. It wasn't until after he left the business that he ever thought about getting into beer.

The brewhouse and fermentation operation at The Olde Mecklenburg Brewery
PHOTO COURTESY OF THE OLDE MECKLENBURG BREWERY

"I was actually camping with my family in Montana," he says. "I had picked up a paper and was reading an article about somebody up in New England working on rebuilding the old Narragansett brewery, and it struck me that there were no breweries in Charlotte. I told my wife that I'd go back to Charlotte and open a brewery, and that's what I did."

When Marrino got home, he began putting his business plan together, then started teaching himself about beer. He converted his garage into a brewery and "bought every book known to man" to figure out how to pursue his new career path. "I figured that if I was going to start a brewery, then I'd better learn how to make beer." A year and a half later, The Olde Mecklenburg Brewery opened its doors.

The brewery focuses on German-style beers, adhering closely to the Reinheitsgebot, the Bavarian Purity Law of 1516, which states that all beer should be made of just barley, water, and hops. "I lived in Germany for four years," says Marrino, "and I just like German beer." That plan proved ideal for his part of the state. Charlotte and Mecklenburg County are both named after Charlotte of Mecklenburg-Strelitz, who became

Queen Charlotte when she married King George III of England. "It fits in with the character of the area," Marrino says of his German beers. He also notes that few breweries focus exclusively on German styles. "Most of the breweries you see out there are making either English- or Belgian-style beers, and I like to be a little different. That's just the way I am."

The Olde Mecklenburg Brewery is noted for its spacious taproom and *Biergarten*, which is open five nights per week and serves traditional German food and, of course, the brewery's German beers. Marrino says

A rare sight of snow at The Olde Mecklenburg Brewery
PHOTO COURTESY OF THE OLDE MECKLENBURG BREWERY

that the taproom was always something he wanted, although it wasn't actually in the business plan. Once it was built and open, it exceeded everything he had hoped for, proving itself to be a popular hangout for the burgeoning craft beer crowd in Charlotte. "It's been a pleasant surprise," he says.

Running the brewery has included "highlight after highlight" for Marrino. "Being able to go out to any one of 220 bars in Charlotte and be able to drink my beer has been pretty great." What's more, he has recently seen his beer in grocery stores, too. Olde Meck introduced bottles in 2011 and plans to expand production in 2012. It is even looking at quadrupling the size of its brewhouse.

Other than that, "we're just going to continue to make Charlotte into a good craft beer location," Marrino says. "We've been making good progress, but we're still only 0.4 percent of the Charlotte market. We still have lots of room to grow."

CHARLOTTE : *Charlotte Oktoberfest*
OKTOBERFEST

12ᵗʰ Annual

- When it happens: October
- Where it happens: Metrolina Expo in Charlotte
- Ticket prices: About $35 for a regular ticket or $50 for "premium" admission
- Features: Beer from 100-plus breweries around the state and country, as well as from Carolina BrewMasters, Charlotte's home-brew club
- Notes: This is one of the best-attended beer festivals in the state. It features a vast array of homebrews.

NoDa Brewing Company

2229 North Davidson Street
Charlotte, NC 28205
704-451-1394
E-mail: info@nodabrewing.com
Website: http://www.nodabrewing.com
Hours: Tuesday–Friday, 4 P.M.–8 P.M.;
   Saturday, 3 P.M.–8 P.M.; Sunday, noon–6 P.M.
Tours: Upon request
Owners: Todd and Suzie Ford
Brewmaster: Todd Ford
Opened: 2011

Regular beer lineup: Hop Drop 'n Roll IPA, Pretty Girl
   Pale Ale, Coco Loco Porter, 26th Street Wit

NoDa, short for North Davidson, is Charlotte's arts district—and the scene of the city's latest wave of craft beer. NoDa Brewing Company, the first of three breweries to open in NoDa, is leading the charge.

Todd and Suzie Ford always enjoyed good craft beer but rarely had the time to enjoy it together. Suzie was a banker in Charlotte and Todd an airline pilot. He flew for Pan Am until the airline

NoDa Brewing Company

ceased operations and then started moving freight for Airborne Express. Todd had been homebrewing since 1995, so when the banking industry took a downturn and Suzie found herself out of work, a possibility arose that they had never considered.

"I didn't ever think about going pro," says Todd about his brewing. "Like the airlines, it's a difficult job to get into and make any money, so you obviously have to like what you're doing. We both enjoyed this, and we've been looking forward to the opportunity to run a business together and spend more time with each other." Todd finally resigned from flying in July 2011 to dedicate himself full-time to the brewery.

Their story is a familiar one. "We started having house parties every six months, and we would give away our beer, and more and more people would tell us, 'You need to start selling this. You need to open a brewery,' " says Suzie. "For the first couple of years, we kind of laughed it off, and then we started thinking, *Well, why not?* So we took our retirement, jumped in with both feet, and haven't looked back."

Finding a place for the brewery ended up being a challenge they hadn't anticipated. They searched for months for the right spot, looking at dozens of potential locations. They had a hard time finding a place that met the criteria set by the city of Charlotte regarding the proximity of churches, schools, and residences. They kept coming back to one site in particular for a variety of reasons: good location, nice feel, lots of room, and only one nearby residence that would alter how they laid out their taproom.

Their brewery is directly across the street from CenterStage@NoDa, a popular theater venue. It is also near Birdsong Brewery, which was just a few months behind NoDa Brewing Company in starting up. The Fords believe their brewery fits into NoDa perfectly. "We feel that brewing is an art," says Suzie, noting that they couldn't have found a more perfect community.

What's more, they're excited to be part of the Charlotte beer scene as it grows. "Charlotte's palate had been expanding, thanks to John Marrino at Olde Meck and Jon Fulcher at Four Friends," says Todd. "People are starting to embrace craft beer. I think Charlotte's on the cusp of seeing the craft market take off."

The Fords assembled a formidable team for their young brewery, hiring George Allen, formerly a brewer for Carolina Beer & Beverage

The brewhouse as seen through the windows behind the bar at NoDa Brewing Company

and Red Oak in North Carolina and Bison in California, as their brewery manager, and two other brewers, Chad Henderson and Matt Virgil.

For now, they're content with opening their brewery. But they're already looking at the possibility of packaging down the road—"probably in cans," says Suzie. "It's the most environmentally friendly packaging, and it's what's best for the beer."

"We're not the youngest people to start a brewery," says Todd. "Everybody gets involved in the industry for different reasons, but we really enjoy the craft beer industry culture—enough so that we basically dumped relatively well-established careers to do it. We both understand that it's going to be a big challenge, and that we're going to make less money at this than what we did before, but we're both dedicated to doing this. It's our passion, and—God willing—I think we'll have some success. I think Charlotte's ready, and all of North Carolina is ready, for some new, unique beers."

BEER AND WESTERN CAROLINA BARBECUE

Western Carolina barbecue bears a few distinctions from eastern Carolina barbecue. Eastern 'cue is made from a whole hog and has a vinegar-based sauce. Western Carolina barbecue is normally just the pork shoulder, which means it's all dark meat—much moister and fattier. And the sauce—even for the coleslaw—includes ketchup. What this means is that western Carolina 'cue is a richer, sweeter experience than its eastern cousin.

A whole different slate of beers pairs with western Carolina barbecue. Try an English-style IPA like Highland's Kashmir IPA or a pale ale like Carolina Brewing Company's Carolina Pale Ale, Highland's St. Therese's Pale Ale, or Foothills' Pilot Mountain Pale Ale. The caramel backbone of each of these beers pairs wonderfully with the pork, and the hop character combats the rich sweetness of the western Carolina meat-and-sauce combo. Be careful of anything that is too hoppy. Intense hop character runs the risk of overwhelming the delicate flavor of the pork (but would probably go great with the coleslaw!).

Foothills Brewing

638 West Fourth Street
Winston-Salem, NC 27101
336-777-3348
E-mail: info@foothillsbrewing.com
Website: http://www.foothillsbrewing.com
Hours: Daily, 11 A.M.–2 A.M.
Owner and brewmaster: Jamie Bartholomaus
Opened: 2004

Regular beer lineup: Salem Gold, Pilot Mountain Pale Ale, Torch
  Pilsner, People's Porter, Hoppyum IPA, Seeing Double IPA

Seasonals: Total Eclipse Stout, Rainbow Trout ESB, Gruffmeister
  Maibock, Sexual Chocolate Imperial Stout, Foothills Red, Hurricane
  Hefeweizen, India Style Brown Ale, Oktoberfest, Foothills Festive,
  German Alt, Scottish Ale, Olde Rabbit's Foot (collaborative brew
  with Olde Hickory Brewery and The Duck-Rabbit Craft Brewery)

Awards: 2007 GABF Silver Medal for "Baltic-Style Porter"
2007 GABF Silver Medal for "Gruffmeister Bock"
2008 World Beer Cup Gold Medal for "People's Porter"
2008 World Beer Cup Silver Medal for "Total Eclipse Stout"
2009 GABF Bronze Medal for "Sexual Chocolate Imperial Stout"
2010 GABF Gold Medal for "Bourbon Barrel Aged Sexual Chocolate
  Imperial Stout"
2010 GABF Bronze Medal for "Foothills Oktoberfest"
2010 World Beer Cup Silver Medal for "Sexual Chocolate Imperial
  Stout"
2011 GABF Silver Medal for "2010 Bourbon Barrel Aged Sexual
  Chocolate Imperial Stout"

Foothills Brewing in Winston-Salem

Jamie Bartholomaus started his brewing career at a young age. He began homebrewing around 18, "maybe 19," as a sophomore in college. He got his start commercially simply by being a good customer. John Gayer, the owner of Blind Man Ales in Athens, Georgia, also ran a homebrew shop, and Jamie was one of his biggest customers. Eventually, he invited Jamie in to help him brew. By the end of 1997—after Jamie graduated from college as an anthropology major—he was brewing at Blind Man full-time.

He still considers his time there to have been some of his most valuable. "It was like large homebrewing equipment. The kettle was a big square tofu cooker with burners on the inside. The mash tun had handmade screens. We only had one pump in the whole facility, so we couldn't do more than one thing at once. We used to bottle out of homebrewing bottling buckets," he says with a laugh. "I learned a lot about what not to do, and how to get stuff done at all costs. Now, when stuff goes wrong, it doesn't really freak me out that much. It's probably happened before."

Jamie enjoyed brewing, but it didn't pay well. Soon after taking the job at Blind Man, he also began to follow his chosen career path, working for Southeast Archaeological Services. He dug at historic sites and brewed on the side.

Soon afterward, a good friend vacated a head brewer's position at Vista Brewpub in Columbia, South Carolina. Jamie jumped at the chance to be a brewer there. But it was "kind of a dead-end brewpub," he recalls. "It was French fine dining, martini bar, raw bar, brewpub. They had a French chef, $25 to $30 entrées. Fine wine is what most people drank, and they had a raw bar right there on the bar." Though it was a fine pl[ace] to work, it didn't move much beer. He continued to brew on the [side] for Blind Man. He worked with Vista for almost four years, all th[e while] looking around for brewery work that would be a better fit for [him.]

On a trip through North Carolina to visit his sister in [...] Jamie stopped into Olde Hickory for a beer and by chanc[e met own]ers, Steve Lyerly and Jason Yates, who were in the proc[ess ...]

Taps lined up at Foothills Brewing

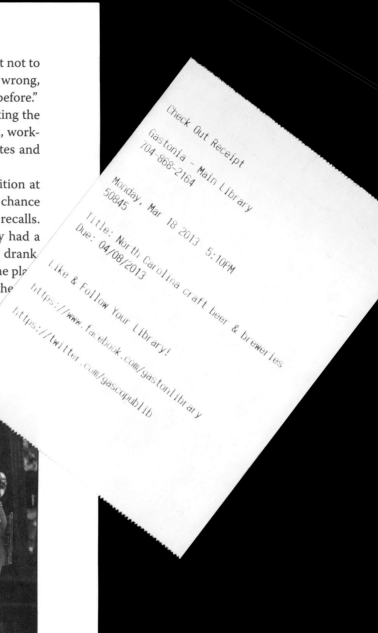

Brewers organizing and cleaning kegs at Foothills Brewing

their production to meet the demands of their new taproom. They needed a brewer. They started asking around after Jamie. Soon afterward, he joined the team at Olde Hickory Brewery, took over production in its Amos Howard's Brewpub, and helped build its production facility.

Jamie worked at Olde Hickory for almost five years, helping the brand grow. Eventually, though, he found himself restless in the job. "Their timeline was different than my timeline," he admits. "I wanted to move at a faster pace than they were committed to. I really wanted the brand to grow." So when some friends had an idea to start a brewpub, Jamie eagerly signed on to the project. Feeling it would be inappropriate to open a brewery near the one where he had been working, he took a job at Blue Ridge Brewing in Greenville, South Carolina, while his project got off the ground.

Finally, in 2005, he moved to Winston-Salem and opened Foothills Brewing, a big, open brewpub with two stories of expansive seating, event space, and a comfortable bar overlooked by tall windows through which customers can see the brewery. At Foothills, Jamie had a brand that he could grow. While the brewpub was the main focus, Jamie started self-distributing the beer. By the end of the year, he had footholds in beer markets around the state.

The distribution and growth of the brand are his passion. "The challenges of getting it made often bring me back to the Blind Man days where at any cost it's got to happen. You know, every year we add equipment, and by the middle of the year we're struggling to keep up, and you can almost predict it. It's a lot of fun to keep up with."

Foothills got to the point where it needed a production facility to meet demand. When Jamie went looking for it, he found an even larger opportunity.

Carolina Beer & Beverage was once a brewery in its own right. In fact, at one point, it was the largest producer of craft beer in North Carolina, thanks to its popular Carolina Blonde and Carolina Strawberry Blonde beers, as well as the Cottonwood brands, which it purchased from Boone's Cottonwood Brewery when it stopped producing beer. Over time, though, Carolina Beer & Beverage found a lucrative side

Sexual Chocolate, one of the most popular beers at Foothills

business—canning energy drinks and bottling progressive adult beverages (like Mike's Hard Lemonade) for distribution. Its brewing operation fell by the wayside. Soon, all the brands owned by Carolina Beer & Beverage were contract-brewed at Pennsylvania's Lion Brewery and merely distributed in North Carolina.

Enter Foothills Brewing. Jamie simply wanted to buy the old brewhouse and fermenters that Carolina Beer & Beverage had sitting around its warehouse. But Carolina Beer had a different idea. "We'll sell you the equipment," they said, "but you have to buy the brands, too."

Now, Jamie's wish for brand growth has met its challenge. At the end of 2011, Foothills completed construction on its new brewing facility. Along with all the Foothills brands he has been growing, Jamie is also now brewing Carolina Blonde, Carolina Strawberry Blonde, and Cottonwood's Endo IPA. The pub, he says, will focus more on special brews, seasonals for the brewpub, and, of course, the popular, award-winning Sexual Chocolate Imperial Stout and the annual collaboration on Olde Rabbit's Foot.

High-value, small-release beers like Sexual Chocolate and Olde Rabbit's Foot are some of the best reasons to visit Foothills Brewing. On the date of their annual releases, beer aficionados from around the United States descend on Winston-Salem, attend the prerelease party at the brewpub to get a sample of the coveted brews, and often spend the night outside just to be the first in line to buy a bottle of the beer the next day.

Liberty Steakhouse & Brewery

914 Mall Loop Road
High Point, NC 27262
336-882-4677
E-mail: libertyhp@tbonz.com
Website: http://www.libertysteakhouseandbrewery.com
Hours: Daily, 11 A.M.–2 A.M.
Tours: Upon request
Owner: T-Bonz Restaurant Group
Brewmaster: Todd Isbell
Opened: 2002

Regular beer lineup: Rocket's Red Ale, Nut Brown Ale, Miss
  Liberty Lager, Blackberry Wheat, India Pale Ale, Deep
  River Wheat, Patriot Porter, Oatmeal Stout

Liberty Steakhouse & Brewery is unique in North Carolina
in that it is a stand-alone in a chain of restaurants. It is part
of the T-Bonz chain, based in Charleston, South Carolina. Other
Liberties—in the form of Liberty Tap Room & Grill locations—
exist around South Carolina. The Myrtle Beach location is a brewpub. T-Bonz also operates a full range of seafood restaurants and
cafés in South Carolina. There is only one Liberty Steakhouse &

Liberty Steakhouse & Brewery in High Point

Brewery. It is the sole member of the T-Bonz chain in North Carolina. The other thing that sets it apart is its location just outside High Point, "the Furniture Capital of the World." It stands alongside a mall, where visitors might expect to see an Applebee's, P. F. Chang's, Chili's, or other chain restaurant. Instead, at Liberty, they're greeted with well-made craft beer.

Liberty's first location—in Myrtle Beach—was opened by Josh Quigley in the mid-1990s in conjunction with T-Bonz. Quigley owned a homebrew shop in Charleston, and T-Bonz approached him about the possibility of starting a brewpub. The chain sent him to a short course in brewing at the University of California–Davis and shortly thereafter opened Liberty's first location. Soon, in order to make beer for the other T-Bonz locations, it started another venture in South Carolina, a packaging brewery called New South Brewing.

In the meantime, T-Bonz was working on another Liberty, this one in High Point. Needing a brewer, it hired Eric Lamb, an experienced packaging brewer from Mendocino Brewing Company in Hopland, California. It was a quick change of pace for Lamb, who went from being a large plant packaging brewer to the sole person in a small brewery, creating his own recipes, managing his own procurement, and even helping out behind the bar when needed. Lamb's work ethic and fantastic beer meant that when Josh Quigley left Liberty in Myrtle Beach to start his own brewpub, Quigley's Pint and Plate, Lamb moved to Myrtle Beach to brew there, and a new brewer was brought on in High Point.

That new brewer didn't work out and soon departed the High Point location, which left Lamb brewing at both places, making the long commute between High Point and Myrtle Beach on a regular basis until 2007, when Liberty found Todd Isbell.

Isbell had been around beer since he was a kid. His father worked for Miller Brewing Company in Fulton, New York, not as a brewer but as a production manager. Isbell remembers spending time around the brewery as a child.

He learned about beer while hanging out with his brother in high

Patrons enjoy the bar at Liberty Steakhouse & Brewery.

The brewhouse at Liberty Steakhouse & Brewery

school. They had a ritual. Each weekend, they would pick up a six-pack of Milwaukee's Best and a six-pack of something they had never heard of—an import, a microbrew, something that looked unique. "So, very quickly," he says, "I was able to learn that beer isn't what the Big Three tell you it is."

Isbell learned how to homebrew while he was in college. After that, he went into the army and was stationed in Germany, where his beer education really began. "I was able to learn all about German beer and to see how ingrained into society it was," he says. When he left the army and moved back to the United States, he started homebrewing again. In addition to holding a regular engineering job, he volunteered at Empire Brewing in Syracuse, New York.

"It wasn't much," he says, "just a couple of evenings a week and maybe a weekend day every week." He did that for close to a year and fell in love with it. "I had one of those epiphanies that I guess a lot of people don't ever have, where I realized that money isn't everything and that you have to do what you love."

He immediately started saving up and put himself through UC-Davis's Master of Brewing program, graduating in 2004. He received job offers afterward, but not many he was interested in. "I couldn't just take an entry-level bottling line position or anything," he says. "I still had bills to pay. I had all of these student loans from my first run at college."

His brother lived in Colorado. Knowing that many breweries were located there, Isbell moved. Two weeks later, he got a job at Rock Bottom in Westminster, Colorado. The next two to three years saw Isbell moving through a variety of part-time positions at breweries around Colorado, including Ironwork Brewery. "They never really had a consistent lineup of beers, so I got to play around with recipes a lot," he remembers. "Fear of failure wasn't really present."

In 2007, longing to get back to the East Coast, he saw an advertisement for an open position at Liberty. He did a working interview alongside Lamb, took a look at the area, tried beer from the local breweries, and was sold on the job. By the end of the year, Isbell was brewmaster at Liberty Steakhouse & Brewery.

Like his position at Ironwork, he has the ability to play around in the brewhouse. The Liberty locations in Myrtle Beach and High Point have the same names for many of their beers, but the recipes are those of the individual brewmasters.

Isbell has won dozens of medals at local professional brewing competitions in his few short years at Liberty. He has seen nothing but growth there. "We're officially undersized," he says proudly. "We can't make any more beer with the equipment that I have."

The pub part of Liberty Steakhouse & Brewery reflects its mall location, with its tiled floors and conservative black design. But nothing can take away from the gleaming beauty of the copper brewhouse attached to the side of the pub. Floor-to-ceiling windows let natural light flood the brewery, and sunlight glints off the fermenters and into the rest of the restaurant.

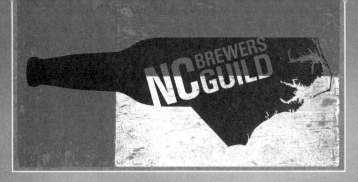

THE NORTH CAROLINA'S BREWER'S GUILD

The North Carolina Brewers Guild is a not-for-profit 501(c)(6) tax-exempt organization comprised of brewers, vendors, retailers, and craft beer enthusiasts focused on promoting North Carolina beer and breweries.

The guild had its start in 2008, when founding members Jamie Bartholomaus of Foothills Brewing, David Gonzalez of Rock Bottom Brewery (now Foothills), Paul Philippon of The Duck-Rabbit Craft Brewery, John Lyda of Highland Brewing Company, and Sebastian Wolfrum of Natty Greene's Pub & Brewing Co. rallied brewers and brewery owners from around the state to a common mission of promoting North Carolina beer, cooperating on purchasing, exchanging knowledge and support among members, and backing—or fighting—legislative initiatives in the common interest of the state's breweries.

In addition, the guild supports and is supported by retail members (bottle shops, bars, and restaurants) and affiliate members (suppliers, vendors, and service providers for the craft brewing industry). It has created an "Enthusiast Program" for North Carolina craft beer fans. Joining the guild as an individual member gets the enthusiast a T-shirt, stickers, and a membership card that entitles him or her to perks at breweries, bars, and restaurants around the state, as well as entrance to special educational events hosted by the guild.

For information, a constantly updated list of North Carolina breweries and their events, and all the latest North Carolina beer news, visit the guild's website at ncbeer.org.

Natty Greene's Pub & Brewing Co.

E-mail: general@nattygreenes.com
Website: http://www.nattygreenes.com
Owners: Chris Lester and Kayne Fisher

Regular beer lineup: Guilford Golden Ale, Buckshot Amber Ale, Southern Pale Ale, Old Town Brown, Wildflower Witbier

Award: 2006 GABF Silver Medal for "Old Town Brown"

Greensboro Elm Street location:

345 South Elm Street
Greensboro, NC 27401
336-274-1373
Hours: Sunday–Wednesday, 11 A.M.–midnight; Thursday–Saturday, 11 A.M.–2 A.M.
Tours: Special occasions only
Brewmaster: Mike Rollinson
Opened: 2004

Seasonals: Red Nose Winter Ale, Dark Horse Belgian Amber Ale, Stamp Act Spring Rye, State House Vienna Lager, Swamp Fox Belgian Blonde, Appalachia Irish Honey Red, Springfest Pilsner, Summerfest Dortmunder Lager, Full Moon American Strong Pale Ale,

Freedom American IPA, Regulator Doppelbock, Diamond Wei-
zenbock, Slam Dunkelweizen, Smoky Mountain Porter, Bayonet
ESB, Hessian Hefeweizen, Old Fort Cascadian Dark Ale

Greensboro Lee Street location:

1918 West Lee Street
Greensboro, NC 27403
336-856-6111
Hours: Daily, 11:30 A.M.–1 A.M.
Tours: Upon request
Brewmaster: Scott Christoffel
Opened: 2006

Seasonals: Red Nose Winter Ale, Black Powder Imperial Stout,
Cannonball Double IPA

Raleigh location:

505 West Jones Street
Raleigh, NC 27603
919-232-2477
Hours: Sunday–Wednesday, 11 A.M.–midnight; Thursday–Saturday,
11 A.M.–2 A.M.
Tours: Special occasions only
Brewmaster: Michael Morris
Opened: 2010

Seasonals: Red Nose Winter Ale, Black Powder Imperial Stout,
Cannonball Double IPA, Hessian Hefeweizen, Smoky Mountain
Porter, Slam Dunkelweizen, Regulator Doppelbock, Stamp Act
Spring Rye

Natty Greene's Pub & Brewing Co. in Greensboro

Back in the early 1990s, Chris Lester and Kayne Fisher were students and friends at UNC-Greensboro, dreaming of one day having their own brewery. In 1996, they finally started down the path when they bought the Spring Garden Bar and Grill, a popular hangout for UNCG students. They renamed it the Old Town Draught House and decided that great food paired with excellent craft beer available at few other locations in North Carolina would be a good fit. The place took off like wildfire.

In 1998, they expanded the idea into Winston-Salem, opening the First Street Draught House. They followed that in 2002 with Tap Room in Greensboro. All three locations followed the same concept: great food, good prices, and excellent beer. In 2004, they acted on their original dream of opening their own brewery. They found a building in downtown Greensboro and renovated it, and Natty Greene's—named after Nathanael Greene, the Revolutionary War general who ran the

Southern Campaign—was born. Although the building they chose was old, it was beautiful and perfectly positioned.

Featuring high-quality food and a suite of beers created by brewmaster Scott Christoffel, the brewpub was an instant hit. Christoffel, a graduate of the Siebel Institute's World Brewing Academy, worked at Left Hand Brewing Company before arriving to create Natty's flagship brands.

The first floor has vaulted ceilings and an enormous dining area that greets patrons as they enter. A dark wooden bar leads toward the brewhouse, which is elevated and sits, gleaming, behind the stairs to the second story. The brewpub also features a quaint outdoor patio and a large event space in the loft that is often used for private parties and business meetings.

It wasn't long before the brewpub started distributing its popular

A view from upstairs at Natty Greene's Pub & Brewing Co. in Greensboro

beers to outside accounts. In fact, Natty Greene's had a difficult time keeping up with production. Lester and Fisher decided it was time to expand. In 2006, they opened a full production facility, hiring classically trained German brewer Sebastian Wolfrum and Mike Rollinson—or "Uncle Mike," as he's known in the brewery. Christoffel moved to the production facility to continue brewing his flagship beers, Rollinson took over the brewpub, and Wolfrum worked as director of brewing operations. With a bottling line and talent in place, the brand exploded. Within three months of opening the production facility, Natty Greene's was the number-one craft beer in Greensboro, outselling all local and national brands.

Soon afterward, the pair decided to expand again, this time in two places.

First came another pub location—this one in Raleigh in the Powerhouse

The bar at Natty Greene's Pub & Brewing Co. in Raleigh

SUMMERTIME BREWS FESTIVAL

Patrons enjoying the Summertime Brews Festival

• When it happens: July
• Where it happens: Greensboro Coliseum
• Ticket price: About $40
• Features: Beer from 100-plus breweries around the state and country, as well as from Battleground Brewers, Greensboro's homebrew club
• Notes: This is one of the few indoor festivals in the state. Visitors will appreciate the air conditioning and excellent bathroom facilities.

148

Square building, the same location as the defunct Southend Brewery. Natty Greene's hired brewer Mike Morris, who had actually started his career brewing in that same building for Southend, then moved on to Capitol City Brewing in Washington, D.C., and Big Boss Brewing Company in Raleigh. The Raleigh brewpub was built to resemble the Greensboro location, with the same dark wooden tones, soft light, and high, vaulted ceilings. However, it is much larger and has more room for the bar, where round tables make up a huge amount of the seating. The Raleigh location also features a game room with televisions, a pool table, shuffleboard, and its own separate bar.

The other expansion was of the production facility, which went from a 6,000-barrels-per-year operation to one that can handle up to 20,000 barrels a year.

Natty Greene's has since continued expanding and has achieved statewide distribution. It hopes to grow even further. Future Natty Greene's pub locations are not out of the question.

Red Oak Brewery

6901 Konica Drive
Whitsett, NC 27377
336-447-2055
E-mail: office@redoakbrewery.com
Website: http://redoakbrewery.com
Hours: Monday–Friday, 9 A.M.–5 P.M.
Tours: Friday at 3 P.M.
Owner: Bill Sherrill
Brewmaster: Chris Buckley
Opened: 1991

Regular beer lineup: Hummin' Bird, Amber Lager, Battlefield
  Bock

Seasonals: Big Oak Vienna Lager, Black Oak Double Bock

In 1979, on a dirt road across the street from Guilford College, Bill Sherrill started his first restaurant. Called Franklin's off Friendly, it was Greensboro's inaugural fine-dining establishment, offering the freshest possible food and a million-dollar wine list. Shortly afterward, Sherrill began opening a chain of restaurants around central North Carolina. The Spring Garden Bar and Grill had locations in Greensboro, Winston-Salem, Charlotte, and Cha-

The brewhouse at Red Oak Brewery

pel Hill. The effort proved to him that the trend toward casual dining was far outstripping fine dining.

Sherrill was no stranger to beer. He had lived a large part of his youth in Europe, graduating from high school in Switzerland and spending time in Cologne, Germany. After college, he experienced the Pacific Northwest and saw firsthand the first microbreweries opening their doors.

He decided to make the switch to casual with Franklin's off Friendly. He closed the restaurant in 1988 and began renovation. Sherrill turned the piano bar into a brewhouse and renamed the establishment Spring Garden Brewery. Its flagship beer was Red Oak, a Vienna-style amber lager created by the original brewmaster at Red Oak, Christian Boos. It was so popular that by 2002, the name of the brewpub was changed from Spring Garden to Red Oak.

Chris Buckley, Red Oak's current brewmaster, grew up in Bonn, Germany, and has the perfect background to work at a brewery specializing in German-style lagers. Through an apprenticeship at one of the oldest breweries in Germany, he is a certified brewer and maltster. He elected to go into brewing rather than malting. "I'm still in contact with most of my fellow graduates," he says of his apprenticeship and brewing program. "There were 27 that graduated that year, and only one went into malting. It's a dusty job, and it's just not as sexy as brewing. At the end of the day, well, a lot of the breweries that you're delivering your malt to will give you beer, but it's not the same as going to your own tanks and getting it directly."

After his apprenticeship, he worked at Paulaner for a couple of years and then moved to the United States, getting a job at Native Brewing Company in Alexandria, Virginia. That job eventually brought him to Red Oak. Both brewing companies used the same German brewing system, so Boos and Buckley were often in touch. "We shared a lot of spare parts," says Buckley, "and we helped each other out in a pinch on more than one occasion. As a matter of fact, when I first took the job, there was still a Post-it note on the desk saying that I had called one day." In 2002, Boos left the brewing industry to take care of a family medical emergency. When he moved back to his native Canada, Red Oak had to look for a brewer.

It employed Henryk Orlik of Abita Brewing Company for a brief stint, but Orlik missed New Orleans and soon had an opportunity to start his own brewery, Heiner Brau, in Louisiana. Left with a German-style brewhouse, an incredibly successful brewpub, and no brewer, Sherrill contacted the brewhouse manufacturer for a recommendation. It put him in touch with Buckley at Native Brewing Company.

For Buckley, the timing was perfect. Native Brewing Company was in the process of moving to Dover, Delaware (becoming Fordham Brewing Company in the process), and it wasn't a shift he was sure he wanted to make. "I came down here and saw the potential for this brewery," he says. "I remember passing those same weathered signs on I-40 that people talked about for years, the ones that said, 'Future Site of Red Oak Brewery.' There was no plan at the time, no blueprints, but I took the job on the premise that they would follow through and actually open up their brewery here."

Buckley soon took over brewing operations at the brewpub. "The brewpub was a fun challenge for me, because I went from working at Paulaner, which was a high-tech, fully automated megabrewery, to Native in Alexandria, which was a semi-automated system, to Red Oak

The bottling line at Red Oak Brewery

in Greensboro, the brewpub, which was entirely manual. It was a real challenge because of the volume that was coming out of there. We had almost 500 accounts. We were doing 16 brews a week, every week. We had just under 1,100 square feet of brewing space, and we made close to 5,000 barrels per year in that facility."

Just a few years later, though, Buckley was able to design, from the ground up, the new brewing facility now in place at Red Oak, in the spot where it had long been advertised. The move to the facility started in April 2007. By July of that year, Red Oak turned out its first batch.

Having closed the brewpub when it made the move, Red Oak is now a state-of-the-art production facility that self-distributes its beers around the state. It started bottling its beers shortly after the production facility opened.

Buckley notes that it's been a bit of a challenge. "We're experts in selling kegs," he says, "but bottles are a totally different market. We make an unfiltered, unpasteurized lager, and when we started pitching bottles to grocery stores, the chains didn't want to keep our bottled beer refrigerated. They all said no. The smaller chains and stores were into it, so we started with them. They care more about what they sell."

Currently, the brewery bottles only one brand—its flagship, Red Oak. Buckley notes that because of the way Red Oak chose to bottle, moving more than one brand is a significant challenge. "All of our bottles are preprinted," he points out. "So, in order to do multiple brands, we would have to have the storage space to hold empty bottles for each single brand, rather than just switching out labels."

In the past few years, Red Oak has finally started to make seasonal beers. It now brews Big Oak each spring and will soon release its first batch of Black Oak, a double bock. But the most exciting thing for Buckley is simply working at Red Oak.

"It's just such a great company," he says. "Around five o'clock, the drivers all start coming back, and there's a huge camaraderie, where we all hang around and talk about the day and talk about new accounts. It's like a big family. We all take pride in what we do, and I think it shows. Running this state-of-the-art brewery is just a dream come true."

THE TRIANGLE

The mash tun being emptied at Carolina Brewery's Pittsboro location

Carolina Brewery

Chapel Hill location:

460 West Franklin Street
Chapel Hill, NC 27516
919-942-1800
Hours: Monday–Thursday, 11 A.M.–midnight; Friday–Saturday, 11:30 A.M.–1 A.M.;
Sunday, 11 A.M.–11 P.M.

Pittsboro location:

120 Lowes Drive #100
Pittsboro, NC 27312
919-545-2330
Hours: Sunday–Thursday, 11 A.M.–11 P.M.; Friday–Saturday, 11 A.M.–midnight

Website: http://www.carolinabrewery.com
Tours: In Pittsboro, first Saturday of each month
Owner: Robert Poitras
Head brewer: Jon Connolly
Opened: 1995

Regular beer lineup: Copperline Amber Ale, Downtown Trolley/Bynum Brown,
Flagship IPA, Oatmeal Porter, Sky Blue Golden Ale

Seasonals/Special Brews: Alter Ego Altbier, Anniversary Ale, Bullpen Pale Ale,
Franklin St. Lager, Jumpin' Java Bean Coffee Stout, Maibock, Oktoberfest,
Old Familiar Barley Wine, Old North State Stout, Phil N. Topemov's Imperial
Stout, Santa's Secret, Super Saaz Imperial Pilsner, To Hell n' Bock, West End/
Circle City Wheat

Award: 2006 GABF Gold Medal for "Flagship IPA"

Carolina Brewery in Chapel Hill

Head west down Franklin Street from the flagship campus of the University of North Carolina in historic Chapel Hill and you'll find the Carolina Brewery, the town's first brewpub, now a major area attraction for beer and food lovers alike.

From the outside, it might be any other restaurant on the west end of Franklin Street. The building features simple brickwork, like many other local businesses. Large maple and pin oak trees grow along the road and push up the brick sidewalk around the tables in the brewery's outdoor dining area. Inside, the proud copper kettle gleams as visitors walk in the door. On most days, the rich, sweet smell of a mash in progress wafts through the restaurant. A long granite bar winds its way around the brewpub just feet from the brewing equipment, so visitors can often listen to the bubbling of active fermentation while watching their favorite sports team on the flat-panel televisions above the bar. The

Carolina Brewery in Pittsboro

upstairs portion of the brewpub is a mixture of comfortable booths, tables, and a private room where patrons gather for seasonal beer releases and other special events.

Owner Robert Poitras was in school at UNC–Chapel Hill when he became entranced by beer. During a semester abroad near Interlaken, Switzerland, he found himself getting to know the area's food and culture. "I was impressed with the sense of pride people had for their local beer," he notes. Afterward, he had a chance to tour other parts of Europe and noticed the same kind of pride elsewhere. Meanwhile, he was experiencing flavor profiles he hadn't been familiar with in America.

When he returned to the United States, he didn't really think of craft beer as a career path—until the next summer, which he spent in San Diego. He noticed the same thing happening there he had witnessed in Europe: local goods, a great sense of pride in the local beers. And they were beers he really enjoyed.

Poitras looks back on a dinner conversation that summer with his original business partner, Chris Rice (who has since moved on), as a catalyst. "You know, a brewpub would work really well back in Chapel Hill," one of them said. When they returned to school in the fall, Poitras started doing research. "I didn't want to be a banker, stuck up on the 57th floor, working nine to six, and stuck in traffic, and wearing a tie," he realized. He and Rice started trying to make a Chapel Hill brewpub a reality.

The next summer, as they moved toward opening, they toured over 100 brewpubs around the country to get ideas and refine their vision. "We took the best parts of each brewery and put them together," Poitras says.

His first brewmaster turned out to be a master stroke. Originally a mechanical and electrical designer, Jon Connolly had always enjoyed good beer. He knew he wanted to be involved in the beer business in some way since his first sip of a hoppy IPA in California in the 1980s. In the 1990s, his wife got a teaching job in Virginia that allowed Connolly some time to figure out what he wanted to do.

"I did a little bit of homebrewing because I had this understanding that you could make this great beer at home, but of course I was doing everything with syrups," he says. "Whoever thought that tasted anything like Anchor Steam didn't know anything about beer. Of course, at that time, we didn't really have the Internet, so I went to the library to find out if there was any sort of education for brewing."

In January 1994, he attended the Siebel Institute in Chicago, enrolling in its concise course in brewing technology. Soon afterward, he was able to join Legend Brewing Company in Richmond, Virginia. "At that time, they were just thrilled to get someone who knew something about beer, and they trained me and I started working," Connolly says. "But as life would have it, two weeks after I started working there, their head brewer gave his two weeks' notice, so within a month I was head brewer, and I learned really fast everything I needed to learn to make a small brewery hum."

A year later, Poitras contacted him to gauge his interest in moving to Chapel Hill and helping start the Carolina Brewery. Connolly had relatives in the area and had been to Chapel Hill on a visit. "I really fell in love with the town," he says. "My kids were still very young then, and I really wanted to raise them in a small town. It was a perfect fit."

Connolly has been there ever since, helping launch the Carolina Brewery and even custom-designing its draft lines and some of its equipment. The brewery was a success from the beginning, winning medals in regional and national competitions and growing in leaps and bounds. It even started to sell beer to other bars and restaurants in the area.

"It started off slowly at first," Connolly says. "A bar in town would just say, 'Please, can I just put your beer on tap?' And it just grew and grew, and after a while we were having a hard time keeping up with both the brewpub and the wholesale accounts."

To meet that demand, Poitras and Connolly opened a second Carolina Brewery location in Pittsboro in 2007. Pittsboro, they thought, was an underserved location. Just off Highway 64, it is equidistant from Chapel Hill, Cary, and Apex—fast-growing parts of North Carolina's Research Triangle.

The Pittsboro location has turned out to be another great success. It brews beer for numerous wholesale accounts around central North Carolina, including a special beer, Bullpen Pale Ale, for a local AAA baseball team, the Durham Bulls.

The Pittsboro brewery looks like an expanded version of the Chapel Hill location, with the same long granite bar. But Pittsboro also has a

Hops are added into the boil at Carolina Brewery.

large dining room and a gorgeous outdoor patio. The brewing equipment is behind a glass wall to keep the noise from the bar, but patrons can still watch the brewing process or join in a monthly tour to see the operation from the inside. Pittsboro also has a side retail space called The Hop Shop, which sells Carolina Brewery merchandise, growlers, and coffee and breakfast items before the restaurant opens. The Pittsboro brewery features live music throughout the year and even hosts its own farmers' market during the summer.

Both locations offer a "Brew Crew" membership that allows patrons to accrue points as they drink and dine. Prizes range from T-shirts to kegs of beer to beer dinners with friends.

The Chapel Hill pub, which now brews beer only for its location, as well as many of the small-batch seasonals, continues to be a hub of activity for Carolina sports fans and beer fans. It remains a vibrant part of the West Franklin Street restaurant scene.

Top of the Hill
Restaurant & Brewery

100 East Franklin Street
Chapel Hill, NC 27514
919-929-8676
E-mail: contactus@topofthehill.com
Website: http://topofthehillrestaurant.com
Hours: Daily, 11 A.M.–2 A.M.
Owner: Scott Maitland
Brewmaster: John Withey
Opened: 1996

Regular beer lineup: Curve Inn Light, Old Well White, Big
   Bertha Brown, Blue Ridge Blueberry Wheat, Ram's Head
   IPA, Lewis Black Imperial Stout

Scott Maitland, founder of Top of the Hill Restaurant & Brewery, credits his time in the military for pushing him down the path of entrepreneurship. His undergraduate schooling was at the United States Military Academy at West Point. "I was in the Gulf War," says Maitland, "and between my experience having the dumbest company commanding officer that I've ever met in the army, and seeing my father get fired from his job after 19 and a half years at the same bank, it sort of cemented the idea in me that I never wanted anybody stupider than me to be in charge of me ever again. I wanted to run my own business because I realized that, societally, we were making this transition from that whole

Top of the Hill Restaurant & Brewery in Chapel Hill

work-30-years-and-retire deal to where we're all kind of our own free agents."

Following advice from some entrepreneurs he met soon after leaving the army, he enrolled in law school instead of business school to get his start. Ironically, he attended law school at UNC–Chapel Hill and is now an adjunct professor of entrepreneurship at UNC's business school.

After a stint as Ross Perot's Florida campaign manager in his run for president, Maitland returned to Chapel Hill. Construction had just started on a new building atop what used to be a gas station at the corner of Franklin and Columbia streets. When the owner announced that the new building would house a T.G.I. Friday's, Maitland balked. "I couldn't stand the thought of a chain restaurant dominating historical downtown Chapel Hill."

He tells his story about how he came around to the idea of a microbrewery: "So I'm studying law in what was then the only coffee shop in Chapel Hill, and I'm reading a *U.S. News & World Report*, and it's about this company in Seattle, Washington, called Starbucks and whether or not they were going to make it, because they had taken this commodity and turned it into a consumer product. And the whole article was talking about how Mrs. Fields did it with cookies, Ben & Jerry's did it with ice cream, Starbucks is now doing it with coffee. You know in those magazines how they usually have the story inside the story? In there was an article that said, 'What's the next food to be gentrified?' And the answer was . . . I don't know. But everywhere these upscale coffee houses were going, this concept called a 'microbrewery' seemed to be doing very well.

"A half-hour later, the owner of the coffee shop comes out and says, 'Folks, I've got bad news. Tonight is actually my last night of business. But don't worry. Two upscale coffee houses are opening up in downtown Chapel Hill in the next two months.' And he used the same term as the magazine, and that's where I had the thought to do this.

"So I went home and—this being 1994 and there not really being an Internet to speak of—I ran a search on LexisNexis for every article written in the past five years mentioning 'microbrewery,' 'brewpub,' whatever."

His search returned 872 articles. After reading 864 of them, he found an article mentioning that the headquarters of *All About Beer* magazine had moved from Boulder, Colorado, to Durham, North Carolina. It was at that point he thought, *I'm going to do this.*

Soon afterward, Maitland teamed up with his best friend from high school, who was a restaurateur, and Daniel Bradford, the editor of *All About Beer*, to make his idea a reality. Over the course of a couple of years, he raised $1.2 million, much of it from the community. A plaque just inside the main doors of the restaurant bears the names of all the original donors.

With Daniel Bradford's help, Maitland decided he wanted to focus on English-style ales for the brewpub. He took out an ad in the British magazine *What's Brewing*, a CAMRA (Campaign for Real Ales) journal. "It's amazing," he says. "My brewer's wife was in a dentist's waiting office, waiting for an appointment, and the dentist happened to be a home-brewer and a member of CAMRA, and had a copy of the magazine in his office. She just opened it up and saw the ad and brought it home."

John Withey started his professional brewing career at Greene King Brewery in Suffolk, England, before joining the iconic Whitbread Brewery. Over the next couple of decades, he worked his way up to head brewer at Whitbread's Sheffield brewery before leaving for a director's position with the Shepherd Neame chain, where he remained until 1991. After a brief run at a pub near Canterbury where he installed a brewery, he followed the "gold rush" to American craft beer, bringing more than 30 years of brewing experience—as well as his own traditional recipes and even his own yeast—to Top of the Hill.

While Maitland was able to get the corner space before it became a T.G.I. Friday's, he discounts the idea that he has established a landmark site. "This location has always been iconic in Chapel Hill," he says. "We just attempt to deliver the kind of quality it deserves."

It is a beautiful restaurant, spanning the entire third floor of the building. Light wood accents the dark, sweeping bar that greets patrons as they enter. Comfortable seating gives them a close-up view of the brewing operation, which is situated neatly behind a glass partition along the entire restaurant. The most popular feature of Top of the Hill, however, is its balcony seating overlooking Franklin and Columbia streets. That intersection is often packed to overflowing during festivals, holidays, and, of course, NCAA basketball championship runs. "My primary driver here—I mean, I love beer and I love food, but my primary driver here is downtown Chapel Hill," Maitland says. "I love it."

In early 2010, Maitland added another dimension to Top of the Hill by opening the Back Bar inside the same building in a space previously occupied by the Carolina Theater. While still showcasing the sleek design of Top of the Hill's brewpub, the Back Bar has much more in common with a traditional British pub. It's a hangout offering finger food, pool tables, dartboards, foosball, televisions, and, as would be fitting in any British pub, cask-conditioned ales. Two beer engines—hand-drawn pumps that pull beer from casks stored at cellar temperature beneath the bar—serve up ale the way it has been done traditionally in the UK for centuries.

Top of the Hill was the first brewery in North Carolina to put its beer in cans. In 2004, at the Craft Brewers Conference in San Diego, Maitland met with a company called Cask, which was just starting to manufacture small canning machines for microbreweries. He was immediately enthralled. "I hate growlers," he says. "I think growlers are an abomination. Why anybody would want to treat their beer like that is beyond me. But cans, I thought, *Fantastic!* I thought, *This will be the replacement of the growler.*"

The brewery at Top of the Hill had some extra capacity, so despite the skepticism of his brewing staff Maitland decided to get a small canning machine. What he later discovered was that the minimum order at that time was 160,000 cans. Having already bought the canning line, he felt he had to make the jump. The brewery created a new brand for it: Leaderboard Trophy Lager. Maitland wasn't immediately interested in getting into grocery stores. Feeling that shelf space was already growing tight for craft beers, he decided to not even compete for that space. Instead, he wanted to shoot for a niche where he had noticed a consistent lack of good beer: golf courses.

The effort was extremely successful—so successful, in fact, that the brewery went through all its excess capacity and ended up falling behind on demand.

"That is what led me to get into distilling," says Maitland. He had decided that he needed to build another brewery to handle the canning operation. But as he put the business plan together, he realized that the profit margin on a packaging brewery was much smaller than on a brewpub. So if he was going to make that jump, he wanted to do so with a much larger brewing facility than he was currently operating. Of course, since it would take awhile for his sales and marketing to catch up with his new production volume, he needed a plan to deal with any excess beer he might have during initial production. He therefore started looking at distilling.

Maitland soon realized that, while all kinds of people are doing craft beer now, very few are doing craft distilling, so he shifted gears and left the idea of a brewery expansion behind. He started working on his idea for a microdistillery in 2006. After years of navigating long-untouched laws and regulations, Topo Distillery is set to open in 2012. It will distill vodka, gin, rum, and bourbon using local and organic agricultural products.

Fullsteam

726 Rigsbee Avenue
Durham, NC 27701
919-682-BEER (2337)
E-mail: sean@fullsteam.ag
Website: http://www.fullsteam.ag
Hours: Monday, 4 P.M.–10 P.M.; Tuesday–Thursday, 4 P.M.–midnight; Friday, 4 P.M.–2 A.M.; Saturday, noon–2 A.M.; Sunday, noon–10 P.M.
Tours: Details available via brewery's website and social media
Owner: Sean Lily Wilson
Brewmaster: Chris Davis
Opened: 2010

Regular beer lineup: Southern Lager, El Toro Cream Ale, Carver Sweet Potato, Rocket Science IPA, Working Man's Lunch

Seasonals: First Frost and Paw Paw (Forager beers); Hogwash Hickory-Smoked Porter and Summer Basil (Southern Apothecary beers)

Sean Lily Wilson had no plans to start a brewery when he was the Pop the Cap spokesman.

"I don't know the exact date," he says, "but when the law was looking like it was going to change, I thought, *I like this. I like the industry. I like the people.*" And he saw an opportunity.

Fullsteam

After the law changed and beer with an alcohol content of over 6 percent was finally allowed in North Carolina, he asked himself, *So the law changed. So what?* He was excited by craft beer and enthused to tell people about it. "You become this evangelist of sorts," he says. "So the mission of Pop the Cap after the law changed became celebrating craft beer in North Carolina. I did beer dinners and tastings, and I did it for fun, with the main goal of spreading the word about North Carolina craft beer and helping to rally and centralize the North Carolina brewers themselves and then, finally, to figure out what I was doing in this space."

Pop the Cap was never really a job for Wilson. He didn't get paid. He talks about it more as a labor of love, but it also turned into a good way for him to get familiar with the industry. *I can do this*, he thought.

"I was kind of a late bloomer getting going on starting my own business," says Wilson, "sort of conceiving this in my mid- to late 30s. And for a business called Fullsteam, it took me quite a while to get it done."

What he felt was missing from the market was a brewery that celebrated local ingredients and Southern agriculture. He had developed his love for Southern seasonal food and drink as a waiter at Magnolia Grill,

A view of the bar at Fullsteam through doors made from tanks at an old Falstaff brewery

the iconic Southern restaurant in Durham, when he was 21. He learned about Southern food traditions and what would grow in the Southern soil. Thinking back to those days, it became obvious to Wilson that this niche wasn't being served in the beer world.

Wilson is not from North Carolina, and some have challenged his championing of Southern ingredients, but he defends himself vehemently. "I've lived in North Carolina longer than any place I have ever lived," he says. "I am raising two daughters who were born here, and I am going to live the rest of my life here. This is home. I am from here."

So Wilson began to close the doors on Pop the Cap and to start work on his brewery. In a case of serendipitous timing, he met Chris Davis at a Pop the Cap beer dinner at the Carolina Brewery in Chapel Hill. The dinner was held to celebrate all the gold medals North Carolina won the year after the law was lifted. As the host of the dinner, Wilson ended up sitting down last. He found himself next to an enthusiastic homebrewer, to whom he talked about his idea for a Southern agricultural brewery. Little did he know that he had met his brewer. "It just clicked," Wilson recalls. "It felt right with Chris. It's not because we're perfect personalities together, because we clash, you know, like we should. But he just *got it.* Later, I got to try his beers, and they were so good from the cobbled-together homebrew system that he had that I thought, *I know that with the right training and equipment that this is the guy."*

Together, they have formed exactly what Wilson envisioned: a brewery that celebrates traditional Southern ingredients. They make a cream ale with corn grits and an amber lager with sweet potatoes. They've made beers with pawpaws, persimmons, and local pears. The names of many of their beers celebrate the South or Southern culture. Their sweet potato beer is called Carver Sweet Potato, after George Washington Carver, the famous inventor and agriculturalist. They have a dark ale named Working Man's Lunch, after the classic Southern fast-food lunch of the 1950s—a MoonPie and an RC Cola. El Toro Cream Ale is named to honor Durham, the Bull City, where the brewery makes its home.

Fullsteam's location in the "DIY District" of Durham is a sight to

The stage at Fullsteam

see. The building is an old Pepsi bottling plant just a couple blocks from Durham Athletic Park, best known as the former home of the Durham Bulls and for the starring role it played in the movie *Bull Durham*. Wilson feels incredibly lucky for the find. "I consider it a series of fortunate events that the area that we are in was ready for a renaissance, and that we found a space that was ready to be that. It took me and Chris a year to find the space that was right for us. We always asked the same two fundamental questions. One, will it fit a forklift? Two, will they show up on a Tuesday? The plan was always to have a community gathering spot and to have a manufacturing environment that would allow us to scale, and luckily enough we found it."

That is a bit of an understatement. The building has bloomed. Artwork lines the walls as patrons walk in through the giant metal door graced with Fullsteam's distinctive backward *F*. The open space in the brewery's taproom (nicknamed "R&D") is filled with picnic tables, Ping-Pong tables, and old-school pinball machines. Behind large wooden doors built from fermentation tanks from the old Falstaff Brewery is a neat, sleek taproom with taps sticking directly out of the brick wall. Large chalkboards on each end display each day's taps and North Carolina guest taps. A strip of dry erase board runs down the center of the bar from one end to the other. Patrons are encouraged to draw on the bar.

The brewery part of Fullsteam is partitioned off from the taproom by a giant glass wall that affords visitors a clear view of the brewing operation, starting front and center with the oddly shaped brewhouse/lautertun, nicknamed "Mir" for its resemblance to a space station. Two rows of fermenters lie beyond the glass wall. Patrons who come early enough in the day can watch brewers at work making new batches of the beer that they're enjoying.

Wilson has plans for the future but is hesitant to lay them out. Fullsteam is, after all, still a young brewery. "We definitely want to package. I'm not sure what that means just yet, but we definitely want to get into some sort of packaging. In terms of our goal, we want to be a landmark brewery for the South. I don't know what that means for the size—if that means small and sought-after or if it means sizable and prominent. We're just getting started. But this is my life now. It's my career, and I want to build a multigenerational brewery. Something that will last longer than just me."

ALL ABOUT BEER MAGAZINE

All About Beer has been a mainstay periodical for beer drinkers and brewers alike for decades. It was first published in 1979 as a pop-culture magazine that celebrated drinking culture. The original editor wrote, in his inaugural editor's note, that tastes in America were trending toward light beers. He promised to keep the content "equally light." Many of the magazine's early issues were filled with babes in bikinis, celebrities, and the kind of drinking man's content found in today's men's magazines.

However, the same year that *All About Beer* began publishing, homebrewing was legalized by the Carter administration, and interest in beer that wasn't so light began to grow. Alongside articles about Mr. Universe and Schlitz, the magazine featured stories about how to make beer, profiles of imported beers from Europe, and articles about the tiny breweries that were popping up all over the country—original craft brewers including New Albion, Sierra Nevada, Anchor, and others.

A recent cover of *All About Beer* magazine

In 1993, the magazine was acquired by Daniel Bradford and moved to Durham. Bradford was already well known in the beer industry. He had worked with Charlie Papazian as a literary agent on his homebrewing manifesto, *The Complete Joy of Homebrewing*. He had spent a decade as marketing director for the American Homebrewers Association, the Institute for Brewing Studies, and Brewers Publications. He was involved in *Zymurgy*, a magazine for homebrewers, and helped launch *New Brewer*, a trade magazine for brewers. He was also the director of the Great American Beer Festival from 1985 through 1991, helping to create the festival and competition as they stand today.

When Bradford took the helm at *All About Beer*, the magazine blossomed with information about craft just as the market was exploding. It covered the growing craft industry with fervor, publishing articles on women in brewing, the early years of "extreme" brewing, and homebrewing, among many other topics. At the same time, Bradford brought more and more of the industry into the *All About Beer* offices. *All About Beer*'s Durham offices became the headquarters of the Brewers Association of America (which

Daniel Bradford, president of *All About Beer* magazine, getting ready to enjoy a beer

merged into the Brewers Association in 2005), the North Carolina Guild of Brewers, and the North American Guild of Beer Writers. By 1996, Bradford and *All About Beer* created the World Beer Festival—a group of annual beer festivals in the style of the Great American Beer Festival. *All About Beer* was instrumental in the effort to raise North Carolina's alcohol cap, acting as the headquarters of the Pop the Cap movement.

All About Beer is now a front runner in the beer industry. It has a distribution of over 35,000 and boasts a readership of well over 130,000. It hosts the World Beer Festival in four cities around the South—Durham; Raleigh; Richmond, Virginia; and Columbia, South Carolina—as well as an annual cask beer festival. Through the festivals, it has raised well over a quarter-million dollars for local charities. The magazine continues to support North Carolina craft beer by hosting educational events at libraries, museums, and other venues.

Bull City Burger and Brewery

107 East Parrish Street
Durham, NC 27701
919-680-2333
E-mail: moocow@bullcityburgerandbrewery.com
Website: http://bullcityburgerandbrewery.com
Hours: Monday–Thursday, 11:11 A.M.–10:00 P.M.;
  Friday–Saturday, 11:11 A.M.–11:00 P.M.
Owner and brewmaster: Seth Gross
Opened: 2011

Regular beer lineup: Parrish St. Pale Ale, Bryant Bridge
  Gateway Ale, "Goat" Bullock Bock, Harvest Ale 2011,
  Pro Bono Publico Porter, Stonewall Jackson Brown Ale,
  Bonnie Brae 60 Shilling Scottish Ale

Seasonal: Hibiscus/Cayenne Scottish Ale

THE BULL STARTS HERE.
  That sentence is painted on the floor just as patrons walk
in the door of Bull City Burger and Brewery, or BCBB, Durham's
newest brewpub. A big red line leads away from the front door,

The welcome sign at Bull City Burger and Brewery

guiding visitors between the small brewery, behind glass on the right, and the brightly lit bar and Enomatic wine machine, on the left. Rustic wooden tables are lined up neatly across the restaurant as patrons walk up to the counter, where they can order some of the best burgers imaginable. To the right of the counter, a ramp leads out the back of the building to a patio full of sturdy picnic tables that find themselves full of patrons on sunny afternoons.

Bull City Burger and Brewery specializes in burgers, tube steaks, and, above anything else, local foods. Almost everything at BCBB is made at BCBB. The meat is ground on-site every day. BCBB makes its own sauerkraut and pickles and cures its own bacon. It even makes its own buns. And of course, it makes all the beer.

Seth Gross, the owner of Bull City, didn't start his career as a brewer. He wanted to go to culinary school, but that didn't fly with his parents, so instead he enrolled at the University of Florida and got a degree in microbiology and genetics. But two weeks after graduation, his passion took over, and he enrolled in the Culinary Institute of America in New York. After graduating from CIA, he moved to Chicago and began cooking in five-star restaurants. But something was happening nearby on Clybourn Avenue in a brand-new brewpub called Goose Island. Chicago's first brewpub, it is now one of the most successful in the country.

"Like every other guy in there, I spent a lot of time bothering Greg Hall, the brewmaster, and I guess he took a liking to me," Gross recalls. Hall needed an assistant, and Gross was exactly what he was looking for: someone good with food, flavors, and cooking who just so happened to have a background in microbiology. Gross started working as assistant brewmaster at Goose Island, and his entire career changed paths. He used his college training to do cell counts and maintain yeast health. Meanwhile, his knowledge of cooking helped him come up with new flavors for beer.

He looks back at the experience with fondness. "That period was some of the most rewarding, backbreaking work I have ever done in my life," he says.

After his tenure at Goose Island, Gross started exploring the world of wine. He became a certified sommelier and traveled extensively, tasting and eating at some of the best restaurants in the world. "Wine has been very, very good to me," he notes.

Gross has experience at every tier of the wine business—except as a winemaker. He has worked in distribution and was one of the owners of Wine Authorities in Durham, a successful retail store. "I love wine, but the thing about wine is that I really couldn't make it myself of any quality. We don't really have the climate for it here in North Carolina, plus I don't really have the patience to wait five years for a red to sort of come around."

It was ultimately Wine Authorities, however, that helped Gross find his way back into beer. He sold his share of the store to his business partner and used the proceeds to start Bull City Burger and Brewery.

"For the most part, startup was pretty easy," says Gross. "What really surprised me was how difficult it was to source local pasture-raised beef. I thought that once I explained the concept to people that farmers would be able to get behind it immediately." What he discovered, however, was that, while he was looking for a few specific cuts of meat, farmers weren't interested in selling parts of cows. They wanted to sell the whole thing. "For a while," he says, "I thought I was going to have to open a butcher shop, too." That's when he found Farmhand Foods, a local company whose sole purpose is to connect farmers with restaurants and retailers interested in using pasture-raised beef. It was win-win. Gross jokingly suggests that he's probably keeping Farmhand Foods open single-handedly. "At times, I've gone through over a thousand pounds of beef in a week."

And finally, there's the beer. Gross notes that his tenure at Goose Island taught him authenticity. "It was a time in the early '90s when that's what people were trying to do: brewing authentic English-style ales. And we did it well. At that time at Goose Island, we were brewing 40 new styles of beer every year, which at that time was unheard of."

He brings that same authenticity to Bull City's beers. They are classic examples of English-style ales, whether milds, bitters, porters, stouts, ESBs, or IPAs. He and brewer Luke Studer work meticulously to have the highest-quality beer available to match their food. "Luke came to me before I had even announced that I was opening a brewery," Gross says.

Studer, a graduate of Vermont's American Brewing Guild, had been working at nearby Triangle Brewing Company when he heard rumors of Gross's plan and approached him about the possibility of working there. "Triangle was wonderful, but I always wanted to work in a brewpub," he says.

Gross found Studer to be an excellent match. "He has been fantastic, hardworking, and reliable, and we have an understanding that we won't make any bad beer."

That doesn't mean they don't play outside the boundaries of style a bit, though. Much like Goose Island, Bull City has been known to throw a bit of food into its beer for good effect. For example, its Hibiscus/Cayenne Scottish Ale tastes so much like you've put a fresh cayenne pepper into your mouth that it comes with a warning from the bartender.

The future is bright for BCBB, but Gross doesn't want to talk about plans too soon. "We're still in our first year," he says, "and I want to make sure we have a solid base under us before we look at any sort of expansion or other future plans. Who knows what will happen?"

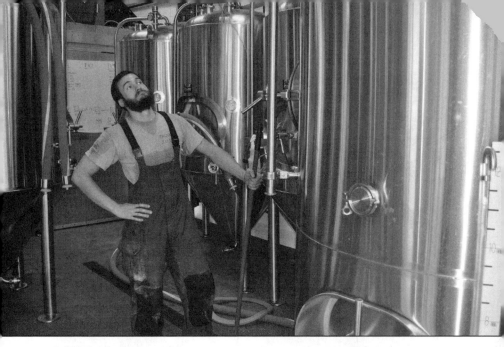

Bull City's Luke Studer

The bar at Bull City Burger and Brewery

Rick Tufts and Andy Miller of Triangle Brewing Company

Triangle Brewing Company

918 Pearl Street
Durham, NC 27713
919-683-BEER (2337)
Website: http://www.trianglebrewery.com
Tours: Saturday at 1 P.M.
Owners: Rick Tufts and Andy Miller
Head Brewer: Rick Tufts
Opened: 2007

Regular beer lineup: Belgian-Style Strong Golden Ale,
  India Pale Ale, Belgian-Style White Ale

Seasonals: Imperial Amber, Mild Ale, Habanero Pale
  Ale, Belgian-Style Lambic, Belgian-Style Abbey
  Dubbel, Bourbon Aged Abbey Dubbel, Xtra-Pale Ale,
  Winter Stout

Rick Tufts and Andy Miller have long been friends, as is obvious to those who meet them. They're quick to poke fun and laugh, especially at the other's expense. That good-natured relationship is at the base of Triangle Brewing Company.

The canning line at Triangle Brewing Company

"Rick and I went to high school together," says Andy. "I came down here for school, and Rick came down and visited a couple of times and kind of fell in love with the area." Rick ended up moving down in the late 1990s to live near his friend. By that point, he was already an avid home-brewer. He got Andy involved in his hobby and his lofty idea to start a brewery. But it wasn't the right time for either of them.

Andy was employed in the hospitality industry. Rick was a psychologist for the University of North Carolina School of Medicine's TEACCH program, working with kids and adults with autism. For the next seven or eight years, the friends continued to spend time together with beer, and especially with homebrew. Finally, they got to a point where it just seemed right.

"My wife told me, 'If you're going to start a brewery, it's got to be right now,' " laughs Rick.

So Rick and Andy sat down and started to think about it in earnest. They decided to take a trip out to the Craft Brewers Conference, which was in Seattle that year, to check out the industry. "To say that we had a good time is probably an understatement," Andy says. "We learned a lot, we met a lot of people, we got a lot of good contact, and more than anything else, we kind of got comfortable with the industry. I think we started our business plan on the plane ride back."

Soon afterward, Rick enrolled in Vermont's American Brewers Guild to learn the craft. He followed that with an apprenticeship at Flying Fish Brewery in Cherry Hill, New Jersey, where he fell in love with Belgian beers. The two friends then worked on getting a brewery going. Since Andy's background was in hospitality, he took care of all the sales and distribution. Rick made the beer and focused on the brewery. It was a match made in heaven.

Originally, they were going to open with a pale ale and an IPA, but after Rick spent time at Flying Fish, he realized that a whole range of beers wasn't typically being made in North Carolina—Belgian-style beers—and that's what they decided to focus on.

"We were told by a few people in the industry that we had lost our minds for having our flagship be Belgian-Style Strong Golden Ale, that it would never work in North Carolina," Andy says. "We're proud to say that a year and a half later, we had 70 accounts and we were looking for a distributor."

They look back with fondness upon the opening of their brewery. "Our first tap ever was the Carolina Ale House in Brier Creek," says Andy. "We sold them a half-barrel of our golden ale for $130, and we were so excited. We played soccer that night on an indoor team, and when the game was over we all went over to the Carolina Ale House and dropped about $300 in beer and food there. The next day, they called us up and said, 'Hey, we need to order another keg. The one you sold just kicked!'" The friends laugh about the irony.

"I still get excited when I see somebody pulling on our tap," says Andy.

"Or going to a store and seeing them looking at your beer and talking about your beer, and then putting a six-pack into their shopping cart," adds Rick. "It never stops being cool."

When taking one of Triangle Brewing Company's tours or attending its Black Friday Cask Festival, hosted every year on the day after Thanksgiving, it's impossible not to notice the small coffin set up somewhere around the brewery. It's not actually a coffin, but a jockey box—a device used to serve beer at events. But the reason it's coffin-shaped is

A view from the stands at the World Beer Festival in Durham Bulls Athletic Park

ALL ABOUT BEER WORLD BEER FESTIVAL, DURHAM

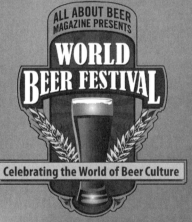

- When it happens: October
- Where it happens: Durham Bulls Athletic Park in Durham
- Ticket prices: About $40 for a regular ticket or $75 for VIP admission
- Features: Exhibiting breweries from around the country, along with most North Carolina breweries; live music; food; educational sessions led by the staff and founders of *All About Beer* magazine
- Notes: Visitors appreciate the easy parking and good access to bathrooms.

very real. The building that Triangle inhabits was built in the 1950s. It has a two-story basement—part that's built out of cement and part that is just natural clay. When the friends were having the building renovated for the brewery, the construction crew found a body partially buried in the clay.

"The bag was obviously tied from the outside," says Rick, "so he didn't put himself there. And the cops weren't able to find anything out about him except that he was a male, just because of his rib structure. There were no dental records back then, no DNA records. So we sat down and we thought, *We've got to name this guy!* We thought that Rufus James sounded like a good Southern name, and now he's the patron saint of Triangle Brewing Company."

"He oversees all aspects of the brewery," Andy adds. "He sees everything. And when he's not happy, things are not good in here—clogged filter, stuck mash, canning line throwing cans at you, whatever. And we pour a little bit of beer down the drain every once in a while to appease him."

Triangle was one of the first breweries in North Carolina to put its beers in cans, and was the first packaging brewery to do so. When asked about what made the partners decide to get into canning, Rick immediately falls back on the trademark joking between the friends. "Well, first and foremost, Andy likes it in the can." After a quick laugh, he turns serious. "But it was really about what was going to be best for the beer, best for the environment, and best for our bottom dollar. It's better for the beer because cans don't let light or oxygen in. And we like to make beer for the drinker on the go, someone that can take a six-pack to wherever they want. And cans travel better—to the beach, to the ballpark, to the mountains, kayaking, anything."

"Look at the extended summers you've got here in North Carolina, and all the pools, where you can't have glass," adds Andy.

Rick has the final word: "First, they thought we were crazy because our flagship is Belgian-Style Strong Golden Ale. Then we were crazy for putting it in cans."

Brewer Ian Van Gundy works on a keg at LoneRider Brewing Company.

LoneRider
Brewing Company

8816 Gulf Court, Suite 100
Raleigh, NC 27617
919-442-8004
Website: http://www.loneriderbeer.com
Hours: Thursday–Friday, 5 P.M.–9 P.M.; Saturday, 2 P.M.–7 P.M.
Tours: By request
Owners: Steve Kramling (VP of brewery operations), Mihir Patel
  (CFO), and Sumit Vohra (CEO)
Head brewer: Ian Van Gundy
Opened: 2008

Regular beer lineup: Shotgun Betty Hefeweizen, Sweet Josie Brown,
  Peacemaker Pale Ale

"Outlaw" releases: Deadeye Jack Porter, Sundance Kid Pilsner

"Most Wanted" releases (22-ounce only): Belle Starr Belgian
  Holiday Ale, Breakfast Stout

"Brew It Forward" releases: Gunslinger Pilsner (Brew It Forward
  1), Grave Robber Black IPA (Brew It Forward 2), Bucking Bronco
  Kölsch (Brew It Forward 3), Brew It Forward 4 (March 3, 2012)

Awards: 2010 GABF Gold Medal for "Sweet Josie Brown"
2011 GABF Silver Medal for "Deadeye Jack"

oneRider Brewing Company is the brainchild of three colleagues: Sumit Vohra, Mihir Patel, and Steve Kramling. All three worked as software quality-assurance engineers at Cisco Systems, Inc., in Research Triangle Park. (In fact, two of them still do.) For a while, they were all on the same floor, within a five-second walk of each other. They've even been on each other's teams at different points in time. To say that they had experience working together would be an understatement.

Kramling and Patel had been homebrewing together when Vohra started working on Kramling's team. "He was just getting into beer at the time," Kramling remembers, "and he was very excited about the homebrew." Together, the three talked about the possibility of opening a brewery, but nothing came of it until a friend let them know that the Mad Boar Brewery in Myrtle Beach, South Carolina, was ending operations and putting its equipment up for sale. They were offered a good deal and decided this was their chance.

Preparations being made for a special keg of brown ale with raspberries

Raspberry juice is squeezed from frozen raspberries
into a special keg of brown ale.

They bought the equipment and found a space in North Raleigh that would accommodate it. Unable to afford a general contractor, they did most of the work themselves on nights and weekends. By November 2008, they were ready to open their doors.

They needed only one thing: a full-time brewer. Kramling was ready to do a lot of brewing, but the trio decided that the best strategy for their bottom line was a staged exit from Cisco. So they set out to find someone who could make beer all day.

Enter Ian Van Gundy, a homebrewer and a student of the craft. In fact, Van Gundy had worked for years at a local homebrew supply store, American Brewmaster, quietly honing his craft until he saved up enough money to head to brewing school. He enrolled in the Siebel Institute's Master of Brewing program and spent the better part of a year in Chicago and Munich learning the best practices in brewing. He returned from his training just in time for LoneRider.

Van Gundy joined the staff and immediately started working on the recipes, building what were already fantastic recipes into brilliant beers that not only showcased their ingredients but were also excellent examples of their styles. In fact, in the three years LoneRider has been open, it has already brought home two medals from the Great American Beer Festival, the largest and most prestigious beer competition in the country.

It might seem odd that a brewery owned by two Indians and their Southern white friend ("I'm the token white guy," Kramling jokes) should be called LoneRider Brewing Company, something that celebrates the Wild West, but there's more to the name than might appear. In their original concept, LoneRider was going to be called Outlaw Brewing Company.

"We're the guys who said, 'We don't want to do what we do. We want to do what we like,' " says Vohra. "It's always something that resonates with everybody. If I asked you, 'Have you ever done something in your life that somebody else thought you shouldn't have done?' the answer is usually yes. There are very few people who say no. In some sort of fashion, every one of us tries to do something different and is some sort of an outlaw."

Their outlaw nature is on full display at the brewery, where their logo—a Clint Eastwood–esque cowboy—graces the side of the building as well as the interior wall just above the beautiful copper-plated brewhouse they received from Mad Boar. LoneRider has grown so much and so quickly that they are completely out of room. The fermenters are squeezed in as tightly as possible, and kegs fill every available space. They had to move their cold room into the taproom—where it looms above the bar and the small wooden tables—to make room for the new bottling line, one of the things that's making their growth possible.

They're looking to upgrade the facility as soon as possible, but they need to find a new space to do it in. They've already outgrown the one they put so much blood, sweat, and tears into just three short years ago. Yet despite all the growth and their happiness with their success, the trio saves their warmest words for the people they've hired. "I think we have the best crew in town," says Vohra. "That's what keeps the brewery running. We're very proud of our team."

POP THE CAP

Until 2005, the definition of a malt beverage in the North Carolina General Statutes read as it had since Prohibition: " 'Malt beverage' means beer, lager, malt liquor, ale, porter, and any other brewed or fermented beverage containing at least one-half percent (0.5%), and not more than six percent (6%) alcohol by volume."

All beer in North Carolina was limited to 6 percent alcohol or less. This policy was instituted when the state legislature passed the Alcoholic Beverage Control Act of 1937. It was never revisited. North Carolinians had few options for beer in 1937, just four short years after Prohibition. Many business owners may have greeted a cap on alcohol in beer as a way to control drunkenness in their workers.

In the 1990s, in the midst of the craft beer revolution, the restriction had a stifling effect on the beer industry in the state. In-state brewers couldn't brew many of the popular styles being produced around the country and the world, and distributors were limited in the beers they could import into the state for resale.

Unfortunately, many people—even those interested in good beer—had no idea a limit was in effect.

Sean Lily Wilson, past president of Pop the Cap, relates how he learned about the law: "A friend of mine from business school took me to a party at Duke back in 2002. In it, they were selling, for a dollar per pint—true pints—barleywines and 'Batch Number-Ones' and cored and caged bottles and things I'd never seen before in North Carolina. I just started asking, 'Why have I never seen this before?' And my friend said, 'Well, they're illegal in North Carolina.' And my reaction was, 'That's really stupid. What can we do about it?' So it kind of got into my head, and I started research-ing, and I realized that North Carolina was one of five states with this restriction, and it just got to me a little bit.

"That night was my craft beer epiphany. I was a craft beer enthusiast just starting to explore this world of craft beer that was unavailable in North Carolina. And up to that point, I thought I knew craft beer really well. You know, I had bought Sam Adams on sale at Harris Teeter, and I supported the few local breweries that were here when I had the chance. But it was from that party that I thought, *Let's figure this out.*"

Wilson contacted Daniel Bradford, the publisher of *All About Beer* magazine. Bradford helped organize the movement. By Feb-ruary 2003, some 35 beer lovers were meeting in the offices of the magazine with one goal in mind: lift the alcohol-by-volume cap on beer in North Carolina.

The effort took two and a half years. The nonprofit organiza-tion, named Pop the Cap, raised money from thousands of North Carolinians in order to hire lobbyist Theresa Kostrzewa, who even-tually shepherded the bill through two House committees, two Senate committees, and both houses of the state legislature. The bill did not pass without argument. It met opposition by those who likened strong beer to "drinking straight vodka" and those who argued that beer with a higher alcoholic content would lead to unwanted pregnancies and academic-related suicides.

In the end, the bill passed both the House and the Senate by comfortable margins and was signed into law by Governor Mike Easley on August 13, 2005—but not without a slight change. The original bill as filed merely removed the cap on alcohol complete-ly. Yet by the time the bill passed the legislature, another artificial cap of 15 percent was imposed, ostensibly to keep the alcohol percentage of beer distinct from that of wine. (Unfortified wine, fermented naturally or with sugar, does not exceed 17 percent al-cohol. Fortified wine, which usually has added brandy to stop the fermentation, exceeds 17 percent alcohol.) However, the new cap effectively limits only a handful of specific beers—mostly ultra-rare novelties—from entering the state.

"In a way, our 15 percent cap makes those rare high-alcohol exceptions all the sweeter to track down and enjoy," Wilson says.

Roth Brewing Company

5907 Triangle Drive
Raleigh, NC 27617
919-782-2099
E-mail: info@rothbrewing.com
Website: http://www.rothbrewing.com
Hours: Monday–Saturday, 4 P.M.–10 P.M.
Tours: Thursday–Saturday at 5 P.M., 7 P.M., and 9 P.M.
Owners: Ryan and Eric Roth
Head Brewer: Eric Roth
Opened: 2010

Regular beer lineup: Raleigh Red, FoeHammer Barleywine, Dark
   Construct

Seasonals: Forgotten Hollow Cinnamon Porter, Mi Mei Honey Plum
   Hefeweizen, Sex Viking Dunkelweiss

Roth Brewing Company holds the distinction of being North Carolina's first nanobrewery.

How small is it? Its kettle makes just two barrels of beer per batch, and its mash tun is so tiny that it looks like something intended for

The brewhouse and fermentation operation at Roth Brewing Company

a restaurant kitchen, not something that creates dozens upon dozens of kegs of beer each month for a commercial brewery. Roth has four-barrel fermenters that stand about as tall as the Roth brothers themselves. In order to fill the fermenters, Roth needs to brew twice. Normally, it does this in one day. In all, Roth brewed over 200 times in its first year of operation. And at the end, it made as much beer as some larger North Carolina craft breweries do in a week. It's a tough business model, but Roth is turning it into a success.

The company is owned and operated by the Roth brothers, Ryan (the CEO) and Eric (the head brewer). They started the brewery almost on a whim. Their first foray into homebrewing was in April 2008, and they were instantly hooked. By December of that year, they had formed their company and were working full speed toward starting a brewery.

"We were probably the least-prepared people to start a brewery ever," jokes Ryan Roth. "We've never worked at a brewery before, we never knew anybody that worked in a brewery, never owned a business, and nobody in our family ever owned a business. Without the resources available online via the SBA and the plethora of books available, we wouldn't be here right now. If we had tried to do this 25 years ago, it

Ryan Roth of Roth Brewing Company

would have been a different story." Ryan's background is in engineering. After graduating from North Carolina State University, he started working in a naval shipyard in Virginia, doing submarine repair for the Department of Defense. But he was miserable at his job. "There was no room for creative engineering," he says. "You can't really try something out or do something new. If you make a mistake when you're repairing a submarine, people can die. You do things by the book."

A brewery, however, gave him room to stretch his wings. "By this point, I guarantee that you could put any size brewhouse into that space and we could make it work."

Eric Roth was, at the time of this writing, still in school at N.C. State, wrapping up a degree in agriculture business management. He plans to graduate in the spring of 2012.

The brothers credit their small-sized operation for their success, saying they essentially interned at their own brewery. They had room for error. "At worst," says Ryan, "we dump two barrels of beer. We haven't done that in a really long time, and I don't think we will again."

The brewery is tucked away among tech companies in the northern end of Research Triangle Park—technically North Raleigh. It sits back off International Drive at the end of a parking lot in a metal garage. Once patrons get inside, though, it stops being part of an industrial park and looks a lot more like a combination pub and party pad.

Roth's taproom is small but inviting. As visitors walk in the door, the first things they see are low-slung couches surrounding a coffee table, an old box television, and a vintage video game system. A few tables dot the floor between the couches and the bar. The room is dark, decorated in black and red. The Roth brothers are friendly young guys who have a penchant for hard rock, role-playing games, and Vikings. They like to have fun, and their taproom shows it.

The brewery is tiny, and the low ceiling in the space makes it look even smaller. Roth's two-barrel brewhouse and four-barrel fermenters fit into a space about the same size as the taproom—just a few hundred square feet. The cold room stretches in back of the fermenters, and kegs line the walls. A workbench sitting kitty-corner to the brewhouse showcases the brothers' woodworking—they make their own tap handles out of ax handles that they drill, sand, and paint on the premises. It all fits into a space about twice the size of a two-car garage.

The Roth brothers don't plan on staying small forever. They want their brewery to last. They are proud to have given it their last name and talk about it being around for years to come. They plan to expand in 2012, right in time for Eric to finish his degree and be able to devote himself full-time to the brewery. They hope to have a much larger brewhouse with bigger—and more—fermenters, which will mean a lot more beer and a lot more fun.

ALL ABOUT BEER
WORLD BEER FESTIVAL,
RALEIGH

- When it happens: April
- Where it happens: Moore Square in downtown Raleigh
- Ticket prices: Around $40 for a regular ticket or $75 for VIP admission
- Features: Exhibiting breweries from around the country, along with most North Carolina breweries; live music; food; educational sessions led by the staff and founders of *All About Beer* magazine
- Notes: Arrive early to find a place to park, and be prepared to walk a good distance to the festival.

A rep from Natty Greene's talks to a festival-goer.

Boylan Bridge Brewpub in front of Raleigh's skyline

The bar at Boylan Bridge Brewpub

Boylan Bridge Brewpub

201 South Boylan Avenue
Raleigh, NC 27603
919-803-8927
E-mail: info@boylanbridge.com
Website: http://boylanbridge.com
Hours: Monday–Wednesday, 11:30 A.M.–midnight; Thursday–Saturday,
   11:30 A.M.–2 A.M.; Sunday, 11:30 A.M.–10 P.M.
Owner: Andrew Leager
Brewmaster: Andy Laco
Opened: 2009

Regular beer lineup: Gantlet Golden Ale, Bruno Bitter, Endless
   Summer Ale, We Support Public Transportation by Rail Pale Ale,
   Pullman Porter, Southbound Stout, Hopped Off the Tracks IPA

Seasonals: Trainspotter Scottish Ale, Polar Bear Winter Warmer

The corner of Hargett and Boylan streets features one of the most spectacular views of downtown Raleigh—a view best seen from the patio of Boylan Bridge Brewpub.

Boylan Bridge is the brainchild of architect and cabinetmaker Andrew Leager, owner of Special Projects, LLC, a custom woodworking and design firm in Raleigh. Leager was a homebrewer for just shy of a decade before opening the brewpub. Drawing a parallel between his beer and his cabinetry, he says he likes to take raw materials and have his way with them.

Appropriately, the brewpub is an architectural masterpiece. It resides in an old metal fabrication and welding shop but no longer bears any resemblance to it whatsoever. The pub is wrapped in floor-to-ceiling windows that allow natural light to flow into and illuminate the space. All the woodwork inside and outside was done by Leager and Special Projects. The brewpub's notable features include a beautiful, sweeping bar, a friendly dining area, and an expansive patio crowned by a gorgeous post-and-beam structure dotted with tables overlooking Raleigh's skyline.

The brewery, visible behind tall double doors in the bar area, is a small seven-barrel brewpub system that Leager bought used from Peckerhead Brewing Company in Douglasville, Georgia.

When Boylan Bridge Brewpub opened in 2009, it sold out of beer in two weeks, forcing it to double its capacity almost instantly. Since then, it has been a local stop for the Boylan Heights crowd and many others who look to enjoy their beer in the beautiful setting Leager has designed.

Boylan Bridge Brewpub looking toward its expansive patio

Big Boss Brewing Company

1249-A Wicker Drive
Raleigh, NC 27604
919-834-0045
E-mail: info@bigbossbrewing.com
Website: http://bigbossbrewing.com
Hours: Monday–Tuesday, 5 P.M.–midnight; Wednesday, 5 P.M.–2 A.M.;
   Thursday, 4 P.M.–2 A.M.; Friday, 2 P.M.–2 A.M.; Saturday, 3 P.M.–2 A.M.
Tours: Second Saturday of each month at 2 P.M.
Owner: Geoff Lamb
Brewmaster: Brad Wynn
Opened: 2007

Regular beer lineup: Hell's Belle, Bad Penny, Angry Angel, Blanco
   Diablo, High Roller

Seasonals: Big Operator, Dicer, Monkey Bizz-ness, Sack Time,
   Harvest Time, Aces & Ates

The building Big Boss Brewing Company occupies has been a
brewery for much longer than Big Boss has been around. In
1996, Tomcat Brewing opened its doors at 1247 Wicker Drive in

The bottling line at Big Boss Brewing Company

Raleigh. A year later, Tomcat closed and was replaced by Pale Ale Brewery, which lasted just two years before being taken over by a brewery out of Pennsylvania, Rock Creek Brewing. With Rock Creek came brewer Brad Wynn. Rock Creek lasted only a couple of years before being bought by Chesapeake Bay Brewing.

When Chesapeake Bay closed in 2003, Wynn was ready with business partner Brian Baker. They bought the old brewery and turned it into Edenton Brewery. Edenton stuck around years longer than its predecessors before Geoff Lamb, a UNC–Chapel Hill grad with a background in corporate law, bought a majority stake in the business in 2007. Lamb and Wynn renamed the brewery once more to reduce the confusion of having it honor a city it didn't reside in. The new name was Big Boss, after one of Edenton's most popular beers. The brewery was also rebranded, using a design aesthetic reflecting Lamb's affinity for World War II aircraft.

Wynn started brewing new beers, as well as old favorites under new names, and Big Boss Brewing Company took off. Within the next few years, it expanded its distribution. Its bottles are now available almost statewide, from Asheville and the mountains through Charlotte and, of course, the Triangle.

The brewery is definitely a large manufacturing environment. On Big Boss's monthly tours, patrons enter through the loading dock. The warehouse spills open in front of them, the brewhouse stands tall on the right-hand side, and the fermentation and bottling operations are nestled into rooms along the back wall. One of the highlights of the space is the attached taproom, which resides upstairs from the brewery and is reachable via an interior staircase as well as an exterior entrance. The taproom is dark and homey. Its wooden booths bear the patina of years of use. Across from the small seating area stands a short bar featuring Big Boss's regular beers, as well as some experimental brews that don't see regular distribution. Other small rooms hold a pool table, a Ping-Pong table, and darts. It is a popular hangout for many locals.

Big Boss has become synonymous with fun outdoor events in Raleigh. Among its regular events are Food Truck Rodeos, during which a vast array of roaming food trucks arrive while Big Boss pours beer, and Casktoberfest, an English-style celebration of a German festival. In 2011, Big Boss hosted the Pan-American Coaster Tossing Championships, a competition in which people compete to see who can throw cardboard coasters the farthest.

Spent grain is taken away from the mash tun at Big Boss Brewing Company.

Patrons wait for a tour to begin at Carolina Brewing Company.

Carolina Brewing Company

140 Thomas Mill Road
Holly Springs, NC 27540
919-557-BEER (2337)
E-mail: carolinabrewing@aol.com
Website: http://www.carolinabrew.com
Hours: Friday, noon–6 P.M.; Saturday, noon–4 P.M.
Tours: Saturday at 1 P.M.
Owners: Joe Zonin, Greg Shuck, Van Smith, and Mark Heath
Brewmaster: Greg Shuck
Opened: 1995

Regular beer lineup: Carolina Pale Ale, Carolina Nut Brown Ale,
   Carolina India Pale

Seasonals: Carolina Spring Bock, Carolina Summer Wheat, Carolina
   Oktoberfest Lager, Carolina Winter Porter, anniversary beers,
   Groundhog Day beers, holiday beers

When Joe Zonin, Greg Shuck, and John Shuck moved to North Carolina, they did so to start a brewery. The friends met at Cornell University in Ithaca, New York, and moved to the Pacific Northwest together. Once there, they fell in love with brewing

Art and plaques decorate the wall in the entryway of Carolina Brewing Company.

culture and small craft breweries and decided they wanted to start their own. Feeling the Pacific Northwest was too crowded for another brewery, they looked elsewhere and finally settled on North Carolina.

"When we moved here from Seattle in 1993, there were 12 breweries in downtown Seattle. There were two in the state of North Carolina," says Joe Zonin.

The friends didn't want to just found a brewery, though. They wanted to do it right. They visited over 100 breweries and took ideas from all of them. And unlike most other breweries in North Carolina at the time, theirs started with all new equipment, including kegs.

They opened their doors and made their first sale on July 3, 1995, to the 42nd St. Oyster Bar in downtown Raleigh, a spot they return to annually for a full beer dinner to celebrate another successful year in business. In 1997, they added their bottling line. "We bought a bottling line that was too big for us, and in a few years when we hit 20 years old and we've increased production, it'll still be too big for us," Zonin says with a laugh. That has meant they've put very little wear and tear on their equipment. On a bottling line that is almost 15 years old, they still see less than a 1 percent loss rate, something most bottling breweries can only dream of.

Despite such a long time in business, Carolina Brewing Company is committed to being a local brewery and a local business. "When we started, we were in three counties," says Zonin, "and today, 16 years later, we're in eight." The partners don't have plans for wide growth. "We might try to add on a few areas occasionally," Zonin says, "but we like to sit back and enjoy it. We're not stressed out trying to grow. We're enjoying ourselves."

Being one of the longest-operating breweries in the state has given the partners the chance to see a large part of the brewing industry grow up around them. "It's fun," says Zonin. "We like the competition. We originally felt like we were competing against British imports. Now, we've got all this other small craft. It's great. The consumer is more interested. It's good for everyone. And we've been thrilled to see that we've actually grown over the past five years, even with all of these breweries opening up."

One of the things Carolina Brewing Company is known for around the state is its iconic logo. "We wanted to use an animal, from lions to tigers to bears," says Zonin. "We considered local animals—dogs, cats, turtles, whatever. We even considered Accidental Yak Brewing Company for a while, but we felt like that had too many bad connotations. We settled on a lion because it's regal and aggressive." The company's original logo had a lion emerging from an eggshell resting on a bed of hops and barley, signifying the birth of the brewery.

Carolina Brewing Company's front entrance leads patrons into a small, informal bar with no taps, a wall full of T-shirts, plaques the brewery has earned from its long commitment to the National Multiple Sclerosis Society, and a picture of beer being drunk from the Stanley Cup. "That's Carolina Pale Ale!" says Zonin, a huge hockey fan. For him, seeing CPA drunk from the Stanley Cup after the Carolina Hurricanes' victory in 2006 was one of the highlights of 16 years of operation.

Past the door adjoining the bar, patrons walk into a full-production brewery. The bottling line looms to the left, large 40- and 80-barrel fermenters stand in a row, and every available space is filled with kegs, bottles, packaging, and ingredients. The 20-barrel brewhouse—the same one the partners have been brewing in since they opened—is at the far left of the brewery, opposite the cold room and the informal tasting area, a small, three-sided bar that stands in front of the taps sticking out of the side of the cold room.

One of the other things the brewery is known for is its weekly tour, conducted every Saturday at 1 P.M. for the past 15 years. During the tour, that informal tasting area is filled with eager patrons. "I do about 95 percent of the tours," says Zonin. "We try to walk the line between fun and technical without being too boring." On average, Carolina Brewing Company hosts between 75 and 100 people on the tour. But on busy days, it can see as many as 250 to 300. "It probably helps that we pour 16-ounce samples for people," jokes Zonin. The tours have helped the brewery build and maintain its fan base in the diverse and growing North Carolina craft beer scene.

A view of the brewhouse and fermenters at Carolina Brewing Company

Aviator Brewing Company

209 Technology Park Lane
Fuquay-Varina, NC 27526
919-567-BEER (2337)
E-mail: info@AviatorBrew.com
Website: http://www.aviatorbrew.com
Hours: Monday–Friday, 3 P.M.–midnight; Saturday–Sunday,
    noon–midnight
Tours: Thursday–Friday, 5 P.M.–8 P.M.; Saturday, 3 P.M.–8 P.M.
Owner: Mark Doble
Opened: 2008

Regular beer lineup: Devils Tramping Ground Tripel, Hogwild
    India Pale, Hotrod Red, Steamhead, Madbeach American
    Wheat

Seasonals: Crazy Pils, Saison de Aviator, Old Bulldog Extra
    Special, McGritty's Scotch Ale, Oktoberbeast, Bonehead
    India Brown, Horsepower Double IPA, Caveman Alt, Frostnip-
    per, Blackmamba Oatmeal Stout

A short drive southwest of Raleigh, in the burgeoning suburb of
Fuquay-Varina, in a small industrial subdivision called Technology Lane, is Aviator Brewing Company. It's a fitting location,
given founder Mark Doble's previous career as a software engineer.

Aviator Brewing Company, including the Aviator limo

Before software, though, there was beer.

Back in the 1980s, Mark and his older brother Jim opened The Brew Shack, a homebrew shop in Tampa, Florida. It did well, and the family wanted to expand to a brewpub.

"My mom is British, and her family had owned pubs all over England and Wales," Mark Doble says, "so she was really focused on getting a pub opened. And my brother really wanted to do the brewing, so we opened a brewpub. I wanted to do a packaging brewery. I wasn't really into the restaurant side of it." The family went on to open Tampa Bay Brewing Company in the city's historic Ybor City neighborhood.

Doble moonlighted at the brewery. But he had just graduated from college and wanted to focus on the career he had been preparing himself for, so he got a job at Hewlett-Packard. He ended up working there for over 15 years.

"But time went on, and I kinda got sick of working there," he says. "I always wanted to come back and start a microbrewery."

At that point, Doble was still in Florida. He did research on distribution laws that would support a packaging brewery in the Sunshine State but felt like they were unfavorable. He therefore decided on North Carolina and its favorable beer laws. "And besides," he says, "with RTP here, if it ever didn't work out, I could always fall back into an engineering job there."

He moved to Fuquay-Varina and bought a hangar at the Triple W

Assorted decorations at Aviator Brewing Company

Airport. At that point, he was still doing software design. "I had a small airplane," says Doble, an amateur pilot, "but the hangar was huge. I used to work out of there, just me, my computer, and my airplane." Brewing was still on his mind, though, and he kept his ear to the ground for equipment.

Eventually, he found a brewhouse in Belmont, California, that "needed some work," so he decided to make a cross-country trip to pick up components of his brewhouse, fermenters, and even dairy tanks. It was a tightly orchestrated trip from one location to another. "I flew on a commercial airline, and an 18-wheeler kind of tracked me across the country. I would rent U-Hauls and drive equipment south to meet him, and then we would off-load stuff. It was crazy. There was literally an inch left in the truck when we packed everything in there."

Finally, he got it all back to his hangar in Fuquay-Varina, and Aviator Brewing Company was born. He rebuilt the equipment he had collected from across the country and started making beer. But he still kept working on software. "I always thought it would be something that supplemented my income," he says. "I'd brew in the hangar, and I'd work my job. I love beer, and I wanted to do *something* with it. But I didn't think it would take off the way it did."

Eventually, Doble had a small bar in the hangar that he operated a few nights a week and for tours. "People just kept coming," he says. Some nights, he had 500 to 600 patrons hanging out. "They would drink all of the beer that I had!" he laughs. "I had a two-tap kegerator, and I was filling old soda kegs off of the bright tanks. I could never keep up." So he decided to grow.

That growth had two phases. The first was a taproom supplied by the brewery in downtown Fuquay-Varina in the old Varina train depot. It's a long, warm space with a 38-foot polished wooden bar, wide-plank floors, and tall ceilings. "It's packed all the time," says Doble. The second phase of growth was a larger brewing facility away from the original airplane hangar, in a space that could better handle a brewery. That space is on Technology Lane.

Now, Doble has room for more fermenters. But he isn't done expanding. His plans include installing a new, larger brewhouse, so he can finally move away from the system he cobbled together out of parts. He has more staff—salespeople and delivery people. A new bottling line has just been set up, so Aviator's beers will soon be available in more than just kegs and growlers. Doble has also opened a barbecue restaurant across the street from the taproom.

"We still can't keep up," he says with a smile. "I can't see that we're doing anything that other breweries aren't doing, but I'm not going to complain."

THE COAST

The Mash House Brewery & Chophouse in Fayetteville

The Mash House Brewery & Chophouse

4150 Sycamore Dairy Road
Fayetteville, NC 28303
910-867-9223
E-mail: gm@themashhouse.com
Website: http://www.themashhouse.com
Hours: Monday–Thursday, 4 P.M.–midnight; Friday, 4 P.M.–2 A.M.;
  Saturday, noon–2 A.M.; Sunday, noon–midnight
General manager: Jennifer Washburn
Brewmaster: Zach Hart
Opened: 2000

Regular beer lineup: Natural Blonde, Hefeweizen, Irish Red,
  India Pale Ale, Brown Porter, Stout

Seasonals: Seasonals and fruit beers rotated

Award: 2001 GABF Silver Medal for "Hoppy Hour IPA"

The Mash House is a member of the Rocky Top Hospitality group, a small North Carolina–based chain owned by Dean Ogan, who was named the 2011 Restaurateur of the Year by the North Carolina Restaurant and Lodging Association. Back in 2000,

A grain silo at The Mash House Brewery & Chophouse

Ogan created The Mash House Brewery & Chophouse in Fayetteville as a cross between fine and casual dining. The menu ranges from gourmet fusion to burgers and sandwiches. The Mash House uses as many North Carolina–grown products as possible and consistently ranks among the best restaurants in Fayetteville.

Brewer Zach Hart is a native of Texas. He began brewing in his backyard and soon found himself volunteering at Big Horn Brewery in Arlington and wondering if making beer was what he wanted to do with his life. After getting his feet under him, he attended the University of California–Davis. He subsequently graduated with a degree in brewing science and engineering and received an offer to brew at a large-scale brewery in Chicago. He turned it down in favor of a job in Fayetteville at a startup called Cross Creek Brewing Company—now The Mash House—where he was given the exciting opportunity of beginning with a blank slate, making all of his own recipes from scratch. Soon afterward, he was rewarded for his decision when he received a Silver Medal at the GABF in one of the most highly populated, and thus difficult, categories: IPA.

Hart brings an eye for quality and creativity to The Mash House, creating a wide array of beers ranging from classic styles to experimental seasonals and fruit beers. Recently, The Mash House added a line of barrel-aged beers, including an imperial stout aged in Jack Daniel's barrels.

Growlers of award-winning Mash House beer

HOW TO BUY BEER

It might seem silly, but buying beer isn't as easy as just picking a bottle off a shelf. Like any other perishable product, beer can go bad. Unpasteurized craft beer (i.e., most of it) has a shelf life of about 90 days and should be kept cold at all times. Unfortunately, due to a lack of shelf space, most beer stores—even the really great ones—keep beer at room temperature, which can severely shorten its life span.

Here are some quick guidelines for making sure the beer you buy is (almost) always awesome:

1. Check for dates on bottles, and make sure you're buying something less than 90 days old. Some high-alcohol beers (over 6 percent), especially dark beers, can age exceptionally well. But as a general rule, beer should be consumed soon after it's made. Hop character diminishes over time, so be sure to buy any hoppy beer as fresh as possible.

2. Never buy beer that has been sitting in direct sunlight. Sunlight (and many fluorescent lights) can cause a photochemical reaction in beer that creates an aroma like skunk urine. Professional tasters call such beer "lightstruck," but almost everybody else calls it "skunky." Clear bottles and green bottles allow beer to become lightstruck in a matter of minutes. Brown bottles are more protective, but prolonged exposure can still cause damage to beer.

3. If you're unsure how old a beer is, hold the bottle up to the light and see what the beer looks like. If it contains flakes or large chunks, the bottle is probably old. Over time, proteins and calcium settle out of the beer and create unsightly flakes in the bottom of the bottle that are fairly easy to stir up. Some beers are meant to be hazy, and some are bottle-conditioned and contain yeast. Yeast should look like a fine dust in the bottom of the bottle.

4. Check the area around the bottle cap for rust or lines of yeast. When beer is bottled, foam pours down the side of the bottle, and

a cap is placed on top. A bottle that hasn't been well rinsed may have yeast or beer residue around the crown that can grow mold or bacteria, which in turn can infect the bottle through the seal of the cap and create unpleasant flavors. If bottles have been stored in a moist environment after bottling, caps can sometimes rust, leaving rust around the lips of the bottles.

5. Check the fill level in bottles. Bottling machines leave a wide variance in fill levels, but beer should always be inside the neck of the bottle to some degree. Exceptionally low fills can be dangerous because of built-up pressure within the necks of bottles, or it can be a sign of a poor cap seal, which means that the beer has either leaked or evaporated from within the bottles, and that the remaining beer is probably sour or infected.

Beers on the shelf at a well-stocked bottle shop

Huske Hardware House in Fayetteville

Huske Hardware House Restaurant & Brewery

405 Hay Street
Fayetteville, NC 28301
910-437-9905
Website: http://www.huskehardware.com
Hours: Monday–Tuesday, 11 A.M.–10 P.M.;
 Wednesday–Thursday, 11 A.M.–midnight;
 Friday–Saturday, 11 A.M.–2 A.M.; Sunday, 11 A.M.–9 P.M.
Owner: Josh Collins
Brewmaster: Mark Fesche
Opened: 1996

Regular beer lineup: Level-Headed German Blonde Ale,
 Impale Ale, Kill-A-Man Irish Red, Farmhouse Ale,
 Sledgehammer Stout

Seasonals: Filthy Kilt Wee Heavy, Consecrator Grand Cru

In 1903, when Benjamin Huske constructed the building that would become his landmark department/hardware store—"the Home Depot of its day," says current owner Josh Collins—out in the middle of nowhere in North Carolina's coastal plain, people thought he was crazy. During the years that followed, it became a center of commerce and eventually the center of what is now downtown Fayetteville. After the store closed in the 1970s, the building hosted a variety of tenants ranging from a furniture store to a jewelry store. In 1996, part of the structure was renovated, and a brewery/restaurant was installed by Dr. William Baggett.

In 2006, Josh Collins and his wife, Tonia, the owners of Blue Moon Café in downtown Fayetteville, saw that the brewery/restaurant was in its waning days and decided to take a shot at it. Josh assembled some friends—his "Band of Brothers," he calls them, all still active-duty Special Ops soldiers—who pooled their savings to buy Huske Hardware House around the end of 2007.

What followed was a long renovation. "It used to look more industrial, with this hard concrete and metal look to it," Josh says. "Now, it's all custom woodwork, all maples and red oaks. All the woodwork is handmade. The brewery was a mess. It had 13 years of low maintenance."

Remnants of the hardware store linger in the building, especially in the brickwork. In some areas, the parapets that were the original exterior walls are still visible.

After a year of work, Josh and Tonia reopened Huske Hardware House. The brewpub is beautiful. It is an enormous open space with warm wooden accents throughout. The main room of the brewery is two stories tall. A mezzanine that seats well over 100 encircles the room. A sheltered brick patio with abundant outdoor seating stands to the left of the restaurant. In the rear of the seating area behind tall glass walls lies the brewhouse and fermentation space. All in all, this is one of the largest brewpubs in the state.

To get their brewing operation going, Josh and Tonia hired Julie Baggett, formerly of Abita Brewing Company and at that time the only female brewmaster in North Carolina. "Julie was awesome," Josh says. "I had a huge stack of résumés, and I interviewed about a dozen brewers. They were all these Gold Medal winners, people with huge amounts of experience. But one of my key questions was, 'Are you willing to compete side by side with guest beers?' " Unlike many brewpubs, Huske offers a wide variety of competitors' beers alongside its own. "She was the only one that said yes," Josh recalls. "She was just the right person to bring in to restore the brewery to its pristine state. She invented the flagship beers that we've stuck with to this day."

Baggett has since moved on. In her place, Josh hired Mark Fesche, formerly of Deschutes Brewery in Oregon. Fesche helped open breweries for a time and was the original brewer at Twin Lakes Brewing Co. in Wilmington, Delaware, and Boylan Bridge Brewpub in Raleigh. He took the mantle of brewmaster from Baggett in 2010 and has been keeping the restaurant in beer since.

One of the noteworthy things about Huske Hardware House is its commitment to the military. Fayetteville has a large military community, being the major city nearest Fort Bragg and Pope Army Airfield. The commitment makes even more sense because of the involvement of Huske's six active-duty partners. "These guys are guys that I've been in combat with," Josh says with reverence. "They're good friends that I trust with my life."

Brewmaster Mark Fesche at work at Huske Hardware House

The bar at Railhouse Brewery

Railhouse Brewery

105 East South Street, Unit C
Aberdeen, NC 28315
910-783-5280
Website: http://www.railhousebrewery.com
Hours: Tuesday–Wednesday, 1 P.M.–6 P.M.;
 Thursday, 1 P.M.–midnight; Friday, 1 P.M.–2 A.M.;
 Saturday, 10 A.M.–2 A.M.
Owners: Mike Ratkowski and Brian Evitts
Brewmaster: Brian Evitts
Opened: 2009

Regular beer lineup: Pale Ale, Brown Ale, Honey Wheat,
 Oatmeal Stout

Mike Ratkowski and Brian Evitts met while working at Ferrellgas, a propane company. They found they had similar backgrounds. They're both ex-military guys—Ratkowski was in the army and Evitts in the navy—and they had complementary skills. "We've always had a real good working relationship," says Ratkowski. "Brian's a real numbers guy—in fact, he just got his MBA from

Fermentation and bright tanks at Railhouse Brewery

N.C. State—and I'm more of a people person, marketing person, operations person."

They discussed going into business together. "We had talked about maybe getting into real estate," Ratkowski says, "and of course the housing market crashed, and that became a poor option."

The epiphany came when they were in Alexandria, Virginia, on a sales call. On their way back, they stopped at an Uno Pizzeria for lunch. "It was raining," says Ratkowski, "so there were all these contractors at the bar drinking and eating lunch, and we noticed that they were all drinking all these craft beers. And I thought, *That's kinda weird, because they seem like blue-collar Bud Light, Miller Lite kinda guys.* I just didn't realize how widespread the craft beer phenomenon had gotten. I actually wrote it on a napkin: 'We should start a brewery.' " They still have that napkin.

Following the sales trip, they started looking for equipment. They found a good deal on a system in Kentucky from the Bowling Green Brewing Company, which was going out of business. Soon, they were looking for a space to install that equipment. They decided on the name Railhouse Brewery several months before they located a space. Through a stroke of luck, they found a spot next to the train depot in Aberdeen, right on the tracks.

"It was a little overwhelming at first," says Ratkowski of their first few months. "We got all the equipment put in here on Easter Sunday— just pallets of hoses and pumps and motors and everything. It took us about three months to get everything up and working."

One of the highlights of their first year in business, says Ratkowski, was seeing the void they filled in the area. They had contemplated the North Raleigh/Zebulon area. What drew them south to Aberdeen were the golf and military communities, both of which, they felt, would provide a good customer base for a new brewery. Ratkowski says, "We didn't realize it at the time, but there are a huge amount of homebrewers in the area. We actually have a homebrew club that we started even before we were open. We have 65 to 70 guys in the homebrew club that get together one Saturday a month, order pizzas, bring samples in, and try beers. The guys in the club are a great volunteer work force." In fact, the partners called on that volunteer work force a few times in the first year to help get their brewery up and running.

The bar at Railhouse Brewery

According to Ratkowski, the future is bright for Railhouse Brewery. But it is also difficult to predict. He and Evitts saw about twice as much growth in their first year as they anticipated, and they've recently picked up a new distributor out of Fayetteville, which will help them grow even more. They're planning to expand into other parts of Railhouse's building when it becomes available. They also hope to see Railhouse beers statewide and maybe even in South Carolina or Virginia. "It's just hard to say where the business will take us right now," Ratkowski says, "but we're having a lot of fun."

Front Street Brewery

9 North Front Street
Wilmington, NC 28401
910-251-1935
E-mail: frontstreetbrewery@gmail.com
Website: http://www.frontstreetbrewery.com
Hours: Daily, 11:30 A.M.–midnight
Tours: Daily, 3 P.M.–5 P.M.
Owner: Tom Harris
Brewmaster: Kevin Kozak
Opened: 1995

Regular beer lineup: Coastal Kölsch, River City Raspberry
   Wheat, Port City IPA, Dram Tree Scottish Ale, Lumina Lager

Seasonals: Milds Davis, 80 Shilling, Oktoberfest

Those walking Front Street in historic downtown Wilmington find it impossible to miss Front Street Brewery. Although the brewery's tall neon sign has been lighting up the street since 1995, the building has been there for 130 years. The brewery occupies Front Street's only freestanding building (alleys are on both sides

People gather outside Front Street Brewery.

of it). Prior to housing the brewery, the building served as a clothing shop and a candy store. "I like to tell people it was a brothel," says Kevin Kozak, Front Street's brewmaster, "but I have no evidence of that whatsoever."

Kozak didn't intend to be a brewer. He just sort of fell into it. "I moved to D.C. after college to live with my sister while I was trying to get into law school," he says. While there, Kozak was introduced to craft beer. His brother-in-law was a homebrewer. Inspired by having great beer around, Kozak started waiting tables at Capitol City Brewing Company in Arlington, Virginia. He spent time learning and chatting with the brewmaster. When an assistant brewer position opened up, he took it. After earning some experience, he moved to a job at Thoroughbreds Grill and Brewing in Leesburg, Virginia, which closed its doors about a

The bar at Front Street Brewery

year later. Finally, he found an opening at Front Street. Upon moving to Wilmington, he fell in love with the area.

Kozak took the helm at Front Street after an extended remodeling closure in 2006. When the brewery reopened, he faced the daunting task of creating all new recipes from scratch for a drinking public that had a decade of expectations. "Basically, they told me to make whatever I wanted, but to include the four flagship beers: Lumina Lager, Port City IPA, River City Raspberry Wheat, and Dram Tree Scottish Ale. It was a little intimidating, but it worked out all right." At the start, the Scottish ale wasn't popular, but then "it just took off." Today, it's one of Front Street's bestsellers. Beyond that, Kozak gets to experiment in the brewery, mostly in the winter. In the summertime, it's all he can do to keep up with the tourist traffic.

Front Street is a gorgeous brewpub full of warm lighting and dark-stained wood. Upon entering, patrons are greeted by the brewery—first the fermenters, then the small Bohemian copper kettle system. Seating radiates from the brewhouse toward the long, dark bar. Toward the back of the space, stairs climb to additional seating. The tall restaurant space is crowned by an ornate skylight that looks up onto the building's top floor, a space used for parties, events, and even the occasional mystery dinner theater.

A piece of lore is connected to Front Street. "The brewery is haunted," says Kozak. "People see things. Weird things happen at night." It seems fitting that the brewery is a stop on the city's "Haunted Pub Crawl." According to Kozak, the building is inhabited by the ghost of Henry Wenzel, a German immigrant who fell to his death while painting the ceiling in the early 1900s. Wenzel's obituary said that he had previously worked as a driver for Palmetto Brewing Company in South Carolina. To Kozak, it all makes sense. "A German immigrant and an old brewery worker? No wonder he sticks around the brewery."

While Front Street Brewery is a model of a successful brewpub, it is nonetheless looking toward further expansion. "We've been talking about the possibility of a production brewery to bottle the flagship brands," says Kozak, "to sell up and down the coast where we still don't see a lot of craft."

LIGHTHOUSE BEER AND WINE FESTIVAL

- When it happens: October
- Where it happens: Lighthouse Beer Festival grounds in Wilmington
- Ticket prices: About $30 for a regular ticket or $45 for VIP admission
- Features: Up to 90 breweries serving well over 200 beers
- Note: This is one of the few festivals in eastern North Carolina and by far the largest.

Lumina Winery & Brewery

6620 Gordon Road #H
Wilmington, NC 28411
910-793-5299
E-mail: info@luminawine.com
Website: http://www.luminawine.com
Hours: Tuesday–Saturday, 11 A.M.–6 P.M.
Owner and brewmaster: Dave Hursey
Opened: 2011

Regular beer lineup: Munich-Style Helles, Bohemian Pilsner,
 Kellerbier, Porter, Summer Ale, Hirsch Jager Autumn Brown Ale,
 Scottish Ale, Raccoon Red Ale, Marzen

Lumina Winery & Brewery, located in a little strip of busi-nesses in Wilmington, is the state's only combination winery and brewery. It's a tiny storefront with a wide selection to satisfy a range of tastes. Lumina carries everything from Green Apple Ries-ling and Blueberry Syrah (made with 100 percent North Carolina blueberries) to German-style lagers and English porters.

Dave Hursey is a native Wilmingtonian who worked on the city's police force for many years until an injury forced him to

Lumina Winery & Brewery in Wilmington

retire. That gave him the freedom to pursue other dreams. He had been making wine at home since 1999 and beer since around 2001. In fact, he had explored the possibility of opening a winery while on the police force, but that was considered a conflict of interest.

Hursey opened Lumina in 2005 in a tiny warehouse space in an industrial zone—one of the few spaces he could find that met the city's zoning requirements. It was only later that he was able to move to a more public storefront, and it was early 2011 when he added beer to his portfolio.

He decided to incorporate beer into the winery as a way to diversify his income. "I like beer better than wine," he says, "and I saw a statistic a few years back that said that 33 percent more people drink beer than wine, so I felt like it was a good way to differentiate myself."

Hursey has no formal training in brewing—"just Charlie Papazian's book," he jokes. He thinks some people try to make brewing harder than it is. "I've been to breweries in Germany, and I've talked to brewmasters to see how they do things," he says. "It's all pretty basic."

Lumina focuses primarily on German-style lagers. Hursey credits the time he spent in Bavaria for his brewery's forte. "It's where I really fell in love with beer," he says. He makes his Bohemian Pilsner with 100 percent floor-malted pilsner malt. His favorite is the traditional German-style Marzen he brewed in March and lagered until his brewery's Oktoberfest celebration in September. "I made another batch close to the date of the party, and you could really tell the difference between the ones that had been lagered all summer and the fresh ones," he recalls. "It was remarkable. The true Marzens tasted so much better."

In the front of Lumina's retail shop, among racks and racks of its wine, patrons will also find homebrewing supplies—yet another way Hursey has found to diversify. He sells area hobbyists ingredients,

The wine selection at Lumina Winery & Brewery

Taps stand in front of wine tanks at **Lumina Winery & Brewery.**

equipment, and beer and wine kits—including kits of some of the beers and wines he makes himself.

Lumina is unrecognizable to anybody looking for a large commercial brewery. In a storeroom behind the tall tanks that hold Lumina's wine, Hursey brews on a small three-kettle setup that makes about 10 gallons of beer at a time using electric submersion heaters, since he has no way of venting propane. His fermenters are plastic buckets and "BetterBottles"—equipment many homebrewers use. His fermentation and lagering are managed by a pair of chest freezers with external temperature controllers.

That doesn't stop him from making professional-grade beer, and a lot of it. Hursey says he normally has about 50 to 70 gallons of beer either fermenting or lagering at any one time. While it's a great deal of work, he doesn't mind. "Beer is my passion," he says. "Wine just pays the bills."

Mother Earth Brewing

311 North Heritage Street
Kinston, NC 28501
252-208-BIER (2437)
E-mail: info@motherearthbrewing.com
Website: http://www.motherearthbrewing.com
Hours: Thursday–Friday, 4 P.M.–10 P.M.; tour days, 1 P.M.–6 P.M.
Tours: First and third Saturday of each month
Owners: Stephen Hill and Trent Mooring
Head brewer: Josh Brewer
Opened: 2009

Regular beer lineup: Endless River Kölsch, Weeping Willow Wit,
   Dark Cloud Munich Dunkel, Sisters of the Moon IPA, Second
   Wind Pale Ale, Sunny Haze Hefeweizen

Seasonals: Tripel Overhead, Tripel Overhead (Bourbon Barrel
   Aged), Old Neighborhood Oatmeal Porter, Silent Night Imperial Stout

Mother Earth Brewing might be one of the most beautiful
packaging breweries patrons will ever see. It is located in
downtown Kinston, a city that was once a center of textile production and is now seeing a revitalization, thanks in no small part to
Mother Earth.

Fresh beer at Mother Earth Brewing

Mother Earth was started by Trent Mooring and his father-in-law, Stephen Hill, both of whom were born and raised in Kinston. Hill had been a homebrewer and a lover of beer in the past but hadn't touched it in years. Mooring had been interested in beer since the first craft beer renaissance of the 1990s, when he clerked in a grocery store that had a good selection of beer. But it wasn't until Hill introduced his new son-in-law to an old family recipe—a "Red Eye," a mixture of beer and spiced tomato juice—that Mooring caught the bug. "I was hooked," says Mooring, who began to try his own hand at homebrewing.

They batted around the idea of starting a business that would combine the passions they held in common: beer, agriculture, and, most importantly, Kinston. They both saw a new business as a wonderful way to give back to their hometown. Soon, they had a plan and went in search of a brewer.

After posting an ad on the website ProBrewer.com, they located

Josh Brewer, who likes to joke about the way he found the brewery. "That's our shtick at beer dinners or events when people ask us how we met. We say we met on Match.com."

Brewer had a long history with beer. Back in 1997, a friend of his had received a homebrew kit for Christmas, and they brewed their first batch of beer together. "That first batch had a whole bunch of muck turning around in the fermenter, and we looked at that and thought that it probably wasn't supposed to be like that, so we dumped that batch in the backyard. But I figured I still wanted to do something with it, so I took the kit from him, and it started from there. He never made another batch of beer in his life, and I kept going."

Brewer worked a few "odds and ends" jobs in the late 1990s. At first, his brewing experience came in dribs and drabs. He used to pass

The brewhouse at Mother Earth Brewing

Mother Earth Brewing in Kinston

a brewpub on his way home from a job at Sears and kept bringing home-brew to the brewer there. After a while, that brewer got to a point where he needed help cleaning kegs, taplines, and even the occasional tank. "I never got to brew there," Brewer remembers, "but I got to put in three or four hours, three days a week."

Finally, he got a job in Georgia as head brewer at Hilton Head Brewing Company, an all-extract seven-barrel brewpub, where he ended up having to do extra work to make beer of the quality he wanted. "It was a good step into brewing," he says, "but it was the most hodgepodge system ever."

While at Hilton Head Brewing Company, he started working part-time at Moon River Brewing Company in nearby Savannah. He calls his time there his "big foot in the door" in the brewing industry. After a couple of years, he moved on. "I got a wild hair to move to Hawaii at that point." He and his fiancée packed up everything they had, sold their cars, and headed to Hawaii. There, Brewer worked as a cellarman for Kona Brewing Co. before buying a defunct bicycle tour business, building it back up, and running it for a few years. Eventually, though, he and his fiancée found themselves back in Georgia, where he picked up exactly where he had left off at Moon River.

A couple years later, Brewer and his now-wife took another step toward every brewer's dream and started their own brewpub, Brewer's, in Beaufort, South Carolina. The concept was a good one—a small brewery with an 80-seat restaurant serving organic food—but they just didn't have enough money, and the restaurant ended up going out of business. Once things settled down, Brewer found the listing on ProBrewer.com. Soon, he was a part of the Mother Earth team and, what's more, in full charge of building the brewery from scratch.

"The cool thing was, I came here before they even bought the building," he says. "Trent and Stephen have the business background and no real brewing background, so everything was up to me. 'What kind of equipment do you want? Where's it going to go? Where's the bottling line going to go? Where does the walk-in go?' I got to do the full design. I was here for the full build-out, and the construction and everything. We have the equipment and the backing to do things the way they're supposed to be done."

The Mother Earth building was actually a suite of businesses—an old drive-through pharmacy, a stable, and a barbecue restaurant. The new owners gutted the building and gave it a completely new life. Today, most of a city block is connected via the building's interior, even though many of the storefronts have been retained. The owners installed large, open windows and cut away portions of the floor, not only to accommodate large brewery tanks but to flood the interior with bright, natural light. The bottling operation rests in what used to be the barbecue restaurant. The canning line is in a gallery "next door," even though they are feet from each other inside. A small, dark barrel room connects the brewery warehouse to the taproom, located in yet another former storefront, this one repainted and redecorated with modern lights, chairs, and a high, white, square bar in the middle of the space. Mother Earth also has a beer garden and a roof deck. A spiral slide taken from an old playground Hill used to visit as a child leads from the upstairs offices to the canning room downstairs. All of the design and renovation was handled by Hill, Mooring, and Brewer. The result is a testament to how well they work together.

They still haven't figured out how to do the "Red Eye," though. Mooring notes that they're still working at it, and getting closer. "We haven't been able to perfect it the way we want it yet. We've done a couple of small batches of it, but we haven't been able to get big batches done. Josh just doesn't want those tomato skins going through his heat exchanger," he says with a laugh. "But it's one of the reasons we wanted to get the canning line, because it doesn't seem like the kind of thing for a bottle."

Brewer is working on creating a cream ale specifically for the "Red Eye," and they've considered dosing cans with the spiced tomato juice while it's being packaged. They're confident they'll get it right eventually.

Mooring predicts a bright future for Mother Earth, but all in due time. "We want to grow to be a regional brewery. We just have to make sure we grow at a controlled pace so that our quality doesn't dip."

BEER AND EASTERN CAROLINA BARBECUE

Eastern Carolina barbecue, to take the romance out of it, is hickory-smoked whole hog with sauce (consisting of vinegar, salt, and red and black pepper) either on the side or drizzled on top. A typical barbecue plate includes coleslaw, hushpuppies, and a choice of many, many sides.

Most barbecue restaurants don't serve beer, but that doesn't mean patrons can't plan to have some with their 'cue at home. Eastern Carolina barbecue basically showcases pork and hickory, the two main flavor components—and they're two flavors beer goes especially well with because of the caramelization that occurs during both smoking and boiling.

Check out brown ales and porters—particularly those with a touch of sweetness that are light on roast—for an excellent pairing with eastern 'cue. LoneRider's Sweet Josie Brown and Big Boss's Bad Penny both pair excellently with pork. For a special treat in the right season, look for Hogwash from Fullsteam, a hickory-smoked porter that pairs intense smoky flavor with the smoke in the 'cue.

The Duck-Rabbit Craft Brewery

4519 West Pine Street
Farmville, NC 27828
252-753-7745
E-mail: info@duckrabbitbrewery.com
Website: http://www.duckrabbitbrewery.com
Hours: Friday, 3 P.M.–7 P.M.
Owner and brewmaster: Paul Philippon
Lead brewer: Matt Cooper
Opened: 2004

Regular beer lineup: Amber Ale, Brown Ale, Porter, Milk Stout

Seasonals: Doppelbock, Marzen, Schwarzbier, Barleywine, Wee
Heavy, Baltic Porter, Rabid Duck Russian Imperial Stout, Olde
Rabbit's Foot (collaborative brew with Foothills Brewing and Olde
Hickory Brewery)

Awards: 2006 GABF Bronze Medal for "Milk Stout"
2009 GABF Gold Medal for "Baltic-Style Porter"
2009 GABF Bronze Medal for "Barrel-Aged Baltic-Style Porter"
2010 World Beer Cup Gold Medal for "Milk Stout"

Tucked away in an industrial warehouse in rural Farmville lies
The Duck-Rabbit Craft Brewery, "the Dark Beer Specialist."

The brewhouse at The Duck-Rabbit Craft Brewery

Farmville, a quaint little town representative of North Carolina's coastal plain, is surrounded by tobacco fields and other farmland just a few miles outside Greenville, the home of East Carolina University.

"Where else would you want to start a brewery but Farmville?" asks Duck-Rabbit founder and brewmaster Paul Philippon, a jovial man with a quick smile and a big laugh. "I didn't want to rent, I wanted to own. And I wanted to own enough real estate so that I never had to move." Philippon's four-acre lot allows him a good deal of room to grow. "It's a very friendly town," he continues, "and they've been very welcoming to us. It means a lot to me."

Duck-Rabbit's emblem, a classic optical illusion made famous by 20th-century philosopher Ludwig Wiggtenstein, is a reference to Philippon's former life as a philosophy professor. After graduate school at the University of Michigan, he took a few teaching jobs. His longest stint was at Eastern Michigan University. But academia was not the life for him. "I love beer, I love brewing beer—and I love philosophy, too! But I could see colleagues of mine who I thought were more talented than me in philosophy struggling to get tenure-track jobs. I saw a lot of people unhappy, and it looked like something that I didn't want to go through." It was time for him to look for an alternate career.

Philippon enrolled in the Siebel Institute in Chicago to learn brewing and never looked back. After Siebel, his career took him on a slow but steady path south: from Brewmasters in Cincinnati, Ohio (now closed), to Pipkin Brewing Co. in Louisville, Kentucky (now Bluegrass Brewing Co.), to Williamsville Brewery in Wilmington, North Carolina (now closed). Finally, in 2004, he achieved his ultimate dream. "The goal was always to open my own brewery," he says, "but I wanted to make sure I was familiar with the industry first. I think that's very important."

Philippon's experience served him well. Though Duck-Rabbit brews on a modestly sized system, it's a strong and successful business with a wide distribution network. Duck-Rabbit beer can be found on tap and in bottles across North Carolina and in many other states, including Georgia, Tennessee, Virginia, and Pennsylvania. That's a significant output for a small-town brewery.

The facility looks like many craft breweries that make the most efficient use of their space. The equipment is squashed together on one side

A brewer cleans up at The Duck-Rabbit Craft Brewery

of the warehouse, while storage—empty cases, kegs, and bottles—fills the rest. The bottling line—the piece of equipment that allows this relatively small brewery to distribute up and down the Atlantic coast—sits with its back against the fermenters. The brewhouse backs up to the loading dock.

The Duck-Rabbit Craft Brewery specializes in dark beers. "I brew what I like," says Philippon of his specialty. It's clear that many others like it, too. Duck-Rabbit's Milk Stout is one of the most decorated beers in North Carolina. It has won a series of medals in local competitions but also has fared well outside North Carolina, having won a Bronze Medal at the 2006 GABF and a Gold Medal at the 2010 World Beer Cup, the largest professional brewing competition in the world.

"I'm proud to have made something that people enjoy," says Philippon. "When I go out to festivals and events, people are coming up to me telling me that they enjoy the beer, and it's been very rewarding."

But he saves his kindest words for employees who have moved on from Duck-Rabbit. "It's bittersweet," he says, "because you feel like you've nurtured them. I feel like Duck-Rabbit has made the brewers who have left here what they are. But to see them move on, to become successful elsewhere, and even start their own breweries—it's what I'm most proud of, that I've been able to make a positive difference in their lives. They will always be a part of Duck-Rabbit."

In 2011, Duck-Rabbit opened its tasting room, a small affair attached to the front of the brewery. A couple of tall, round tables occupy space next to the short, sleek wooden bar, which sports four Duck-Rabbit taps. Tall windows and a glass door look into the brewery and offer a close-up view of fermentation vessels. Outside, a picnic table waits to greet patrons on warm Farmville afternoons.

Weeping Radish Farm Brewery

6810 Caratoke Highway
Grandy, NC 27947
252-491-5205
Website: http://weepingradish.com
Hours: Tuesday–Saturday, 11 A.M.–4 P.M.; Sunday, noon–4 P.M.
Tours: Wednesday at 11 A.M., or self-guided during
  business hours
Owner and brewmaster: Uli Bennewitz
Opened: 1986

Regular beer lineup: Corolla Gold, Fest, Black Radish,
  OBX Kölsch, IPA 25, Radler

Seasonal: Winter Doppelbock

Award: 1990 GABF Silver Medal for "Hopfen Helles"

"**I**'ve been here since 1980. I'm a German immigrant," says Uli Bennewitz, founder of Weeping Radish. "I came here to farm, and I still farm. Farming is my life." When Uli moved to North Carolina and Hyde County, he worked as a farm manager,

Goats greet visitors at Weeping Radish Farm Brewery in Grandy.

becoming the only resident on a 30,000-acre farm. "We had 60 miles of roads that I was in charge of patrolling," he remembers. "It was what you expect pioneering to be."

The trouble was that he never really thought farm management would be sufficient for paying the bills and raising a family. In 1985, Uli's brother—who lived in Munich—called him with an idea. He had a friend with a brewery that was up for sale and asked if Uli was interested in buying it.

"I was not very enthralled with American beers at the time," says Uli. "Your choices were either Bud or Coors, which was no choice at all." He immediately agreed to his brother's plan, subject to Uli's finding the capital to enable him to buy the brewery.

He remembers talking to the owner of The Christmas Shop in Man-

A view of the brewery from above at Weeping Radish

teo, a popular tourist destination. The owner told Uli that the question he was most often asked in his shop was, "Is there someplace to eat?" So the two got together, pooled their resources, and decided to open a sandwich stand and brewery.

At that point, after he had already committed to the brewery, Uli faced his first real stumbling block. "I didn't know what the ABC was. I thought it was some sort of learning center. Coming from Germany, I never thought that in the land of the free there would ever be such a thing as an alcohol control board," he says, referring to the state's Alcoholic Beverage Control commission. He met with the ABC and told it of his plan to open a brewery/restaurant. The board broke the news to him that it was illegal. However, the ABC thought it was a great idea and proposed to help him get the law changed.

Soon afterward, Uli began meeting regularly with the chief legal counsel of the ABC drafting the new law, which flew through the legislature in the hands of then–freshman senator Marc Basnight, becoming law just six months after Uli first approached the ABC with his question. Weeping Radish opened on July 4, 1986.

Interestingly, Uli doesn't take full credit for the law change. "It was really Biltmore that did the share of the work," he says. In 1980, Biltmore Estate Winery in Asheville wanted the ability to serve its own wine on the premises, which was illegal at the time. Using its considerable resources, Biltmore had pursued a change in the law for wine. "When I came along, we just used the exact same argument, but we just changed the word *wine* to *beer*," Uli says jovially. "I've always wondered if Biltmore knows that it is essentially responsible for the microbrewery boom in North Carolina."

Weeping Radish, now legal, did not see instant success. "You do not open a brewpub in a dry town," says Uli. At the time, liquor was outlawed in Manteo. Although beer and wine were technically legal, they were frowned upon. "It's a dumb concept. They were not amused to have a brewery in town." Furthermore, the idea behind Weeping Radish was not immediately popular with the local clientele. "Don't open a Bavarian-themed restaurant in the South. There aren't any Bavarian-themed restaurants in the South, and there's a reason—nobody wants one. We did great in the summer when tourists from Midwestern states—Ohio, Wisconsin, Minnesota, Iowa—were in town, but the rest of the year it was dead."

Still, Uli continued to pursue his idea. In 1988, he opened a Weeping Radish in downtown Durham near the Brightleaf Square area. "It was gorgeous. It was a beautiful building with great architecture, and it was a beautiful brewery, but it was about 25 years ahead of schedule." Uli notes that if he opened the Durham location today, it would likely be immensely popular. As it was, it lasted for about a year and a half and then shut down. The city was just not ready.

Back in Manteo, Weeping Radish ran into a new problem. In 2000, the brewhouse fell through the floor of the brewery. "We had an all-wooden structure," says Uli, "a heavy, water-intensive operation on a wood floor."

At that point, he decided to take the brewery to the next level. He had long been interested in the local food movement and was begin-

Stained glass above the counter at Weeping Radish

ning to realize the connection between natural beer and natural food. "They're both crafts," he says. "Beer is a craft, meat is a craft, vegetables are a craft. They're all the same."

After taking a look at the market, he realized there were no craft butchers in the entirety of North Carolina. He then put out an ad in a German journal for a master butcher and began his plans for a full farmhouse brewery in Currituck County. "Literally, all I had was a field," he says. He constructed a 20,000-square-foot building, which he calls "a celebration of craft brewing, butchering, and organic farming—all of these wrapped into one concept."

The building is immense and impressive. Visitors enter an enormous room with a restaurant at the far end. A rough wooden outdoor façade stands over a short bar decorated with newspaper articles about the Outer Banks in the early 20th century. Although the brewing operation is out of sight from visiting patrons, they can take a tour that allows them to see the brewpub-sized brewhouse tucked into an enormous cavern of a brewery. "My real goal," says Uli, "was to have a distillery as a

A view of the bar inside Weeping Radish

companion to the brewery, but the bureaucrats won on that one." Outside, visitors can see fields stretching in back of the brewery. Those are the fields Uli farms. He fertilizes them with waste from the brewery, including spilled beer. In fact, he calls the fields "the first true beer garden in America, without a table, without a chair, without a patron."

In 2011, Weeping Radish's Doppelbock was the first beer in the state to feature 100 percent North Carolina–grown and –malted ingredients. Uli is a supporter of Asheville's Riverbend Malt House, a new craft maltster using all North Carolina–grown barley. "We want to end up growing our own barley and have Riverbend malt it for us," Uli says, "so that we can have a complete closed loop, even more integrated into the farming operation." He notes that he has many more ideas about how to combine beer and food. "There's a lot going on in both worlds that we want to explore."

Full Moon Café & Brewery

208 Queen Elizabeth Street
Manteo, NC 27954
252-473-MOON (6666)
E-mail: fullmoonmanteo@msn.com
Website: http://www.thefullmooncafe.com/gallery.html
Hours: During tourist season, noon–10 P.M.;
    off-season hours vary
Owners: Paul Charron and Sharon Enoch
Brewmaster: Paul Charron
Opened: 2011

Full Moon, nestled in the middle of historic Manteo, has been around since Paul Charron and Sharon Enoch started their café in 1995. At the time, it was a small sandwich shop serving tourists during Manteo's busy season. Soon, though, the café started expanding into the shops around it, creating a larger and larger presence. Enoch even opened a small pottery gallery next door.

Through that time, Charron—a former airline pilot and a longtime disciple of great beer—was homebrewing. "The batches just kept getting bigger and bigger," he says. That's when he considered making beer for the café.

Full Moon Café & Brewery in Manteo

"I thought we could just make one beer and put it on tap, and we could probably make it in the kitchen," says Charron. "We don't really get year-round business, so I figured we could carry all North Carolina beer, and ours would be a complement. But we were quickly overwhelmed."

They decided to open a small brewery in the space that was once Enoch's pottery gallery. And so their brewery was born. It uses a "Brutus Ten" system that Charron built with plans from *Brew Your Own* magazine and small Blichmann fermenters. He currently has the ability to make about one barrel of beer at a time. "I'm overjoyed to say that it is way too small," he says. "We haven't even advertised. We just put a sign up outside, and we can't keep up."

Charron came to the industry with no professional credentials. "It's all homebrew experience," he says. "People come in all the time and ask if I'm the brewmaster, and I tell them, 'No, I'm the guy who brews the beer, but I'm not the brewmaster.' I have an enormous amount of respect for guys with loads of schooling." He notes that the brewers from the other area breweries—Weeping Radish and Outer Banks Brewing Station—were "beyond helpful" while he was getting his brewery up and running. In fact, they are even planning to come over to brew with him in the winter—"the slow season."

Charron currently brews and ferments in the same room that serves as his tasting room and pub. It's a small taproom with a bright, polished copper bar gleaming in front of the brew kettles and fermenters. Full Moon doesn't have temperature control like most large breweries. "We've got central air and some other air-conditioning units," Charron says. In the summer, it gets hot. "Sometimes, to try to control temperature, we have to brew at three and four o'clock in the morning, when it's cool outside and easier to keep the room cool."

Down the road, Charron hopes for continued success. But his plans are really only to supply his own café. Plans for the next year include expanding from a one-barrel system to a two-barrel system and increasing the fermentation space. "If it keeps going this way," he says, "I'd like to move to a bigger site and move up to a seven-barrel system and just brew for the restaurant."

A view of the taps at Full Moon Café & Brewery

Outer Banks Brewing Station in Kill Devil Hills

AMERICA'S FIRST WIND POWERED BREW PUB

OUTER BANKS BREWING STATION
MP 8½ • KILL DEVIL HILLS, NORTH CAROLINA • WWW.OBBREWING.COM

Outer Banks Brewing Station

600 South Croatan Highway
Kill Devil Hills, NC 27948
252-449-BREW (2739)
Website: http://obbrewing.com
Hours: Monday–Thursday, opens at 3 P.M.;
  Friday–Sunday, opens at 11:30 A.M.
Owners: Eric Reece and Aubrey Davis
Brewmaster: Scott Meyer
Opened: 2001

Regular beer lineup: Olsch, Standard Issue Pale Ale, Conquest IPA,
  Abracadabra Brown Ale, Briney-Deep Porter, Dog House Tripel

Seasonal: LemonGrass Wheat Ale

Awards: 2002 GABF Bronze Medal for "LemonGrass Wheat"
2006 World Beer Cup Bronze Medal for "Smolder Bock"
2010 World Beer Cup Silver Medal for "LemonGrass Wheat"

On an island in the Atlantic Ocean, just a few hundred yards from where the Wright brothers' home-built flying machine made the first controlled, powered, and sustained human flights, is the Outer Banks Brewing Station. It's hard to miss.

The bar at Outer Banks Brewing Station

The large red-and-white building stands out among the businesses surrounding it on the main strip of the island, and a wind turbine—taking advantage of the blustery winds on the northern Outer Banks—looms overhead.

Head brewer Scott Meyer has been involved in fermentation for a long time. He was working as a vintner in the wine industry in Northern California when he started seeing tap handles in bars from new breweries—microbreweries. Intrigued, he sought out a local microbrewery—Bison Brewing—and started volunteering and learning how it all worked. He was hooked.

Soon afterward, the head brewer and assistant brewer both left the company, and Meyer was promoted to head brewer. He hired Eric Reece—a lab tech at nearby Bear Technologies—as an assistant brewer. Or, as Reece puts it, "I tasted Scott's beers, and I quit my job."

As luck would have it, though, Bison Brewing (now Bison Organic) was bought out, and the new owners were brewers. Meyer and Reece found themselves out of their jobs. Meyer went back to the wine industry, and Reece went with him, working at Rosenblum Cellars.

Meanwhile, Aubrey Davis, an old friend of Reece's, got tired of his job. Soon afterward, he convinced Reece to return to an idea they had come up with while they were in Thailand in the Peace Corps together: starting a brewpub.

Davis had grown up visiting his grandparents' house on the Outer Banks. He felt it would be the perfect location—and it was, except for actually getting everything built.

"It's hard to find contractors out here," says Meyer, echoing Reece's early frustrations. "Plumbers and electricians don't move out here to work. They move out here to surf or to fish. They'll get work done, but they're doing it on beach time, and nobody's really prepared for any sort

The comfortable entrance of Outer Banks Brewing Station

of industrial setting. These are residential guys that are here for the lifestyle. It's hard to fault them, though. When you live in paradise, it kind of infects you."

Eventually, they got their brewery built—all except for the windmill, which was in the original business plan. It took five and a half years of fighting with the city's mayor and zoning board before they finally got it through. Now, as the state of North Carolina considers a wind farm offshore, the Brewing Station's turbine already offsets about 8 percent of its power needs. "It would be a lot more if we didn't have a brewery," says Reece, "but then we wouldn't have the great beer."

When Reece and Davis opened the brewery, they called Meyer to see if he was interested in helping them. Meyer eagerly accepted. They've been together ever since.

The brewing system is an amalgam of used equipment. They found a brewery in foreclosure and got a trailer full of equipment. In fact, they ended up selling equipment they didn't need in order to finance the rest of what they required. The result is a quirky brewery tucked into a seemingly impossibly small space away from the restaurant. Patrons can see it from the dining room. It is situated half a story below floor level and stands two stories tall. A catwalk runs across the brewery at restaurant level. The only entrances to the brewhouse are outside around the back of the restaurant and a secret-wall-type access through the back of the cold room.

Brewing on the Outer Banks poses some interesting challenges, says Meyer. "The water is horrible out here." He jokingly refers to it as "the three threads of the Outer Banks," in reference to traditional beer in England, which was a blend of three different types of ale. "What we have is basically a mix of desalinated ocean water, water from a coastal aquifer, and good ol' swamp water. The blend changes constantly, and I can't get a reliable idea of what the water is like, chemically, until weeks after the blend changes. So we just strip it down entirely and rebuild it using brewing salts."

The salt air also poses a problem for the brewery, corroding motors and any metal that has to spend time outside. "We have to keep a close eye on our air compressor," says Meyer. "If we don't change the filter about once a month, the entire thing becomes jammed up with salt crystals."

The final challenge is the seasonality. Both Meyer, the brewer, and Reece, the owner, talk about the challenges of having such an intensely seasonal customer base. For Reece, the issue is making sure they capitalize on the four months of tourism to keep the restaurant and brewery open the rest of the year. For Meyer, it's making sure he can keep up with beer production when tourists are in town. "It's not just seasonal," Meyer says. "We actually see fluctuations week to week on the rental schedule. It's impossible to predict what one week will bring over another."

The restaurant is magnificent. It boasts vaulted ceilings and a long, beautiful bar running the length of its back half. "What really sets us apart," Reece says, "is that we care about the food." In fact, Reece's wife, Christina McKenzie, a graduate of the California Culinary Institute, works in the restaurant as well. "You've got to try her carrot cake," says Reece. "It'll make you cry."

The Brewing Station has been in operation over a decade now. Its continued success is a testament to the determination and skill of the old friends. "We have to continually try to reinvent ourselves to keep things fresh," Reece says. "Scott is always trying to find new flavors in the beer, and he's constantly dialing things in, and we do the same with the food, or with entertainment and events. We're very involved in the community, and we like to try to keep the community involved with us. It's very important to us."

Breweries Opening in North Carolina

Since 2005, when Pop the Cap was passed, an almost constant stream of breweries has opened in North Carolina. The rate of openings has increased over the past few years. At the time of this writing, the following breweries were in the planning stages in North Carolina.

Altamont Brewing Company
1042 Haywood Road
Asheville, NC 28806
828-575-2400
http://www.altamontbrewingcompany.com

Beggar's Brewing Company
Mooresville, NC
704-519-6325
http://beggarsbrewing.com

Birdsong Brewery
2315 North Davidson Street
Charlotte, NC 28205
http://birdsongbrewing.com

Cape Fear Brewery
550 October Drive
Willow Spring, NC 27592
919-639-8136

Birdsong Brewery

Dry County Brewing Company
615 Oak Avenue
Spruce Pine, NC 28705
828-765-4583
http://www.drycountybrewing.com/

Golden Cock Brewing Company (GCBNC)
7008 Queensberry Drive
Charlotte, NC 28226
980-422-6463
http://goldencockbrewery.com

Haw River Farmhouse Ales
P.O. Box 390
Saxapahaw, NC 27340
919-741-9039
http://www.hawriverales.com

Headwaters Brewing Company
P.O. Box 311
Waynesville, NC 28786
828-593-8679
http://www.headwatersbrewingco.com

Heist Brewery
2901 North Davidson Street
Charlotte, NC 28205
603-969-8012
http://heistbrewery.com

HomeGrown Brewing Company
3804 Waldenbrook Road
Greensboro, NC 27407
336-580-4558

Ivory Tower Brewery at the Broyhill Inn
Appalachian State University
775 Bodenheimer Drive
Boone, NC 28607
828-262-2204

Liquid Loaf Brewing Company
404 Columbia Drive
Raleigh, NC 27604
http://www.liquidloaf.com

Lost Colony Brewing Company
Holly Springs, NC
http://www.lostcolonybrewing.com

Mucklerat Brew Works
13200 Strickland Road, Suite 114-293
Raleigh, NC 27613
919-802-1778

Mystery Brewing Company
437 Dimmocks Mill Road, Suite 41
Hillsborough, NC 27278
919-MYSTERY (697-8379)
http://www.mysterybrewing.com

Thirsty Monk South
20 Gala Drive
Asheville, NC 28803
828-505-4564
http://monkpub.com

White Star Beer Company
Lexington, NC

Appendix 2
North Carolina Meaderies and Cideries

Beer and wine aren't the only fermented beverages in North Carolina. The state also has a small but quickly growing mead and cider industry. Currently, hard (a.k.a. alcoholic) cider is available at only one spot in North Carolina. But given the growing industry and the long history cider has in the United States, it's hard to imagine that it will be the only one for long. Mead—traditional honey wine—is new to North Carolina but has been well received. Expect to see new meaderies opening over the next few years around the state.

Desi's Dew Meadery
8902 Charlotte Mountain Road
Rougemont, NC 27572
919-732-2808
http://www.ncagr.gov/ncproducts/ShowSite.asp?ID=1757

Fox Hill Meadery
33 Selby Court
Marshall, NC 28753
828-683-3387
http://www.foxhillmead.com

McRitchie Winery & Ciderworks
315 Thurmond PO Road
Thurmond, NC 28683
336-874-3003
http://www.mcritchiewine.com

Starrlight Mead
480 Hillsboro Street, Suite 1000
Pittsboro, NC 27312
919-533-6314
http://starrlightmead.com

Appendix 3
Contract Breweries in North Carolina

Contract breweries are companies that hire someone to brew beer for them. Once the beer is brewed, they either act as their own distributors or hire distributors to sell and deliver the beer for them. Contract breweries tend to get a bad rap because of the misconception that they are not involved in the brewing of the beer. In fact, many contract breweries have their own recipes. Most are closely involved with the brewing process but simply do not own brewing facilities.

Boone Brewing Company/Blowing Rock Ales
P.O. Box 2678
Blowing Rock, NC 28605
828-773-9491
http://www.boonebrewing.com
Brewed at Lion Brewing Company, Wilkes-Barre, PA

Bottle Tree Beer Company
10 North Trade Street, Suite D
Tryon, NC 28782
864-266-0133
http://www.bottletree.net
Brewed at Thomas Creek Brewing Company, Greenville, SC

Good Vibes Brewing Company
3933 Fawn Creek Drive
Wilmington, NC 28409
910-274-2258
http://www.goodvibesbrew.com
Brewed at Thomas Creek Brewing Company, Greenville, SC

Kind Beers
6010 McDaniel Lane, Suite B
Charlotte, NC 28213
704-819-4913
http://www.kindbeers.com
Brewed at Thomas Creek Brewing Company, Greenville, SC

Wolf Beer Company
200 Willard Street
Wilmington, NC 28401
910-763-8586
http://www.wolfbeerco.com
Brewed at Lion Brewing Company, Wilkes-Barre, PA

Appendix 4
Bottle Shops

Bottle shops are, simply put, beer stores. These can be dedicated craft beer bottle shops, wine stores that also carry excellent craft selections, or stores that just happen to have an owner with available shelf space and a passion for craft beer.

The following are some of the absolute best outlets in North Carolina to buy craft beer. Entries marked with an asterisk are must-visit places for any fan of beer.

The Mountains

Adventures in Wine and Beer
205 Thompson Street
Hendersonville, NC 28792
828-693-3939
http://adventuresinwineandbeer.com

Bruisin' Ales*
66 Broadway Street, Suite 1
Asheville, NC 28801
828-252-8999
http://www.bruisin-ales.com

Gail's Hops and Grapes
2420 North Center Street
Hickory, NC 28601
828-267-2672
http://www.gails-hops-and-grapes.com

Hops and Vines
797 Haywood Road, Suite 100
Asheville, NC 28806
828-252-5275
http://www.hopsandvines.net

La Bouteille
10 North Trade Street
Tryon, NC 28782
828-859-6473
http://www.labouteille.net

Peabody's Wine & Beer Merchants
1104 NC 105 South
Boone, NC 28607
828-264-9476
http://www.peabodyswineandbeer.com

Rabbit & Co.
124 Fourth Avenue East
Hendersonville, NC 28792
828-692-6100

The Piedmont

Bestway*
2113 Walker Avenue
Greensboro, NC 27403
336-272-4264

The Bottle Shoppe
174 West Main Avenue
Gastonia, NC 28052
704-810-9463
http://www.thebottleshoppe.biz

Brawley's Beverage
4620 Park Road
Charlotte, NC 28209
704-521-1300
http://www.brawleysbeverage.com

The Brewer's Kettle*
2505 North Main Street, #101
High Point, NC 27262
336-885-0099
http://www.thebrewerskettle.com

City Beverage*
915 Burke Street
Winston-Salem, NC 27101
336-722-2774
http://www.citybeverage.com

The Common Market
2007 Commonwealth Avenue
Charlotte, NC 28205
704-334-6209
http://commonmarketisgood.com

Vintner Wine Market
8128 Providence Road, #500
Charlotte, NC 28277
704-543-9909
http://www.vintnerwinemarketnc.com

The Triangle

A1 Brews
112 Millstead Drive
Mebane, NC 27302
919-568-8880

Barley & Vine
5910 Duraleigh Road, #141
Raleigh, NC 27612
919-235-0018
http://www.barleyandvine.com

The Beer Dispensary*
103 East Chatham Street
Apex, NC 27502
919-267-6040
http://www.thebeerdispensary.com

Bottle Revolution*
4025 Lake Boone Trail, Suite #105
Raleigh, NC 27607
919-885-4677
http://www.bottlerevolution.com

Carrboro Beverage Company
102 East Main Street
Carrboro, NC 27510
919-942-3116
http://www.carrborobeverage.com

East Wake Wines & Craft Brew
1001 Wide Waters Parkway
Knightdale, NC 27545
919-217-1129
http://www.eastwakewines.com

Hope Valley Bottle Shop
4711 Hope Valley Road, Suite 4E
Durham, NC 27707
919-403-5200
http://www.hvbottleshop.com

Kegs and Kans
2908 North Main Street
Fuquay-Varina, NC 27526
919-552-2028
http://kegsandkans.com

Parker & Otis
112 South Duke Street
Durham, NC 27701
919-683-3200
http://parkerandotis.com

Peace Street Market
804 West Peace Street
Raleigh, NC 27605
919-834-7070

Sam's Quik Shop*
1605 Erwin Road
Durham, NC 27705
919-286-4110
http://samsquikshop.com

Tasty Beverage Company*
327 West Davie Street, Suite 106
Raleigh, NC 27601
828-692-6100
http://tastybeverageco.com

TJ's Beverage and Tobacco
306 East Main Street
Carrboro, NC 27510
919-968-5000
http://www.tjsbeverageandtobacco.com

Triangle Wine Company
3735 Davis Drive
Morrisville, NC 27560
919-462-1912
http://www.trianglewinecompany.com

The Coast

Cape Fear Wine and Beer*
139 North Front Street
Wilmington, NC 28401
910-763-3377
http://www.capefearwineandbeer.net

Chip's Wine and Beer Market
2200 North Croatan Highway
Kill Devil Hills, NC 27948
252-449-8229
http://www.chipswinemarket.com

Cindirene's Southern Emporium
559 Third Street
Ayden, NC 28513
252-746-9222

Grapes and Hops
5407 Ramsey Street, #C
Fayetteville, NC 28311
910-822-8700
http://www.grapesandhops.net

Harrika's Brew Haus
911 Cedar Point Boulevard
Swansboro, NC 28584
252-354-7911
http://www.teaandbeer.com

Home Brew Haus
1201 US 70 East
New Bern, NC 28560
252-636-8970
http://www.homebrewhaus.biz

Lighthouse Beer & Wine
220 Causeway Drive
Wrightsville Beach, NC 28480
910-256-8622
http://www.lighthousebeerandwine.com

Zillie's Island Pantry
538 Back Road
Ocracoke, NC 27960
252-928-9036
http://www.zilliespantry.com

Glossary

Adjunct: A non-barley source of fermentable sugar.

Ale: A beer made with ale yeast.

Barrel: Also written as bbl. One barrel of beer contains 31 gallons.

Brewery: The entire building in which beer is made.

Brewhouse: The set of equipment used in the "hot side" of brewing beer: mashing, lautering, and boiling.

Brewpub: A combination brewery and restaurant.

Bright tank: A tank that is used to carbonate beer.

CAMRA: The Campaign for Real Ales, a movement in Britain dating to the 1970s. Its aim is to return tradition to the way beer is served, focusing primarily on cask-conditioned and bottle-conditioned beers. For information, visit camra.org.uk.

Cask-conditioned: Refers to beer that has been refermented in the cask. Cask-conditioned beer is typically served at cellar temperature via gravity or hand pump

CIP: Clean in place. This generally refers to brewery tanks equipped with spray valves that can be used to pump water and cleaning solution to quickly clean the entire tank with little manual labor.

Cold room: A large walk-in (or sometimes drive-in) refrigerator.

Ester: A chemical compound formed during fermentation. Esters often taste fruity.

Fermenter: A vessel in which beer is fermented, where yeasts eat sugars to create ethanol and CO_2.

GABF: Great American Beer Festival, a yearly beer festival sponsored by the Brewers Association in Denver, Colorado. It includes the largest professional brewing competition in the United States.

Growler: A refillable glass jug for beer, often with a screw top, sometimes with a ceramic swing-top. In North Carolina, growlers can hold only 64 ounces (a half-gallon) or less.

Hops: The flower and fruiting body of the plant *Humulus lupulus*, used by brewers to impart both bitterness and flavor to beer.

Kegerator: A refrigerator built to hold kegs and serve beer.

Lager: Literally, "to store." In beer, it refers to beer made with lager yeast.

Lautering: The step in the brewing process in which sugar is removed from grain in order to make the wort.

Lautertun: The vessel in the brewhouse in which lautering takes place.

Malt: Grain, usually barley, that has been slightly germinated and then kilned, creating a reserve of sugars and enzymes. Malt is the source of sugar in beer.

Maltster: A company that malts barley for use in brewing.

Mash tun: The vessel in the brewhouse in which the mashing process takes place.

Mashing: The step in the brewing process when water is added to grain in order to activate enzymes that will convert starch into sugar.

Microbrewery: A brewery that makes 15,000 barrels of beer per year or less.

Nanobrewery: A brewery that makes extremely small batches of beer. While there is no official definition of what constitutes a nanobrewery, it is generally considered to be a brewery that makes batches of three barrels or less.

Reinheitsgebot: The Bavarian Purity Law of 1516, which stated that beer could be made from only three ingredients: water, barley, and hops. Yeast wasn't discovered for another 340 years and so was not included in the law. The Reinheitsgebot also defined a rigorous pricing schedule for beer that is no longer observed.

Sparging: The act of rinsing grain with hot water during lautering, which assists in removing sugars from the grain.

Taproom: A small beer bar often attached to, or associated with, a brewery.

World Beer Cup: The largest international professional brewing competition in the world, it is held every two years, on even-numbered years.

Wort: Unfermented beer.

Yeast: A unicellular fungus that eats sugar and secretes CO_2 and ethanol, as well as hundreds of flavor compounds, in beer.

Index